Gifts from the Train Station:

Healing Yourself by Helping Others

by

Glenn Croston, PhD

This book tells the stories of 14 individuals who have faced life-altering challenges and overcome them, building new lives of hope and renewal by working to help others. Their stories are examples of the greater good we can achieve for ourselves by reaching out for the greater good of others.

Reading Material appropriate for all Adults.

A website and non-profit organization accompany these efforts: www.giftsfromthetrainstation.org

Acknowledgements

This is not your ordinary book to read, and writing it has been a unique experience as well. Sharing what these people have been through has been trying at times, and exhilarating as well as the pieces have come together. Overall, it has helped me see and learn once again, for the umpteenth time in my life, how much we need help from each other and how we can flourish by working together.

This book would not have happened without the help of many people, particularly Rob. Rob got the whole Gifts project started by bravely sharing his story, a step that was not easy I know, but that also seemed essential for him, and for which I am deeply grateful. He has supported and guided this book patiently through all of its many ups and downs as the book revealed what it was meant to be. My daughter Gaia delivered great insight and editing also, helping these stories to shine, and carry their message step by step outward.

And of course I owe the greatest of thanks to all of the people in this book who reached out to share their stories with me, with you, and with the world. Their bravery, heart, and wisdom continue to amaze me every time I read their stories. I've read them many times now, and will probably read them many times more, because I just don't get tired of stories like these that deliver hope and inspiration. I've got a feeling that you can't have too much hope and inspiration in this life.

Thank you for reading – I hope these stories come to mean for you what they have meant for me, making a positive difference in your life.

Table of Contents

Introduction: Beginnings

My friend Rob is recovering from leukemia. He's doing far better now, thank goodness, but for a long time it wasn't fun, particularly for him. He disappeared from work just after Christmas a few years back, falling out of sight like a rock dropped in a pond. At first I had no idea what had happened to him. Did he leave the company? Did he leave the country? He was always somewhat private and a little mysterious. He was from Kentucky and there were rumors of moonshiners, of Harlan County-type justice and a bank robber or two in the family. So, leaving the country was in the realm of possibilities for my PhD-educated friend. My mind tried to follow the ripples, getting nowhere. It was a mystery until the word got out that it wasn't some cheesy 1980s movie plot; he was seriously ill with cancer. No one knew if we would ever see him again. He was going through at least four rounds of intense chemotherapy followed by a bone marrow transplant, if possible. The odds were not in his favor.

It was touch-and-go for Rob for a time. He teetered on the edge before starting to navigate the long road back, a road he still travels with periodic flare-ups of graft-versus-host disease (GVHD) and a small side of skin cancer stemming from the immunosuppressants he needs to take.

Eighteen months later, after Rob was through the worst of it and back to work, we were sitting in his office one day talking when he said a funny thing to me. He said that as bad as all of it was – and it was pretty bad at times – he wouldn't change it. If someone gave him a magic wand or a time machine, he wouldn't take away the cancer, the chemo, and the rest of what he'd gone through because of all that the illness and healing process had given him.

To be honest, I didn't really have a clue what he was talking about. Rob had changed after everything he'd been through and he seemed more at peace with many things. I was glad to see him doing better as his health improved, and it sounded like he was onto something profound, but how on Earth could anyone in their right mind say they were glad they had been through leukemia and a bone marrow transplant, and all of the nastiness that goes with such things? It seemed a little out there. Frankly, it seemed way out there.

But then another funny thing happened. I started meeting person after person saying the same thing. They had been through the full range of life traumas from cancer to car accidents to heart-lung transplants, but at their core their stories were the same. These people had lived through the worst-case scenarios – the kinds of things we sometimes worry about when we lie awake at night. And then, no matter how they had been hurt, no matter what they had been through, they told the universe "Thank you". As hard as they had fallen, they got up, dusted themselves off, and were glad for the trip.

This was worth digging into, to figure out what was going on. The more I looked and the more I listened, the more I began to understand what Rob and the others were saying. I started to get it. After they had seen their old life swept away, they knew deep in their souls that they had been given a second chance. And when you get a second chance, you don't want to blow it. They knew they had to do something that mattered. And they didn't just consider it – they did it. They found ways to reach out to the people around them. They went on to reach people all over the world that needed consolation, encouragement, and a sense that they were not alone – that there is hope. And, in doing so, people like Rob discovered that this outreach also helped them to heal their own scars and build brighter futures for themselves as well.

Hearing the same thing from so many different people, and seeing it in their eyes, I knew this was a story worth telling, a story that needs to be told, because what happened to these people can happen to any of us. It happens every day.

There's no telling when or where it will happen, but nobody gets through this life without hitting some sort of adversity or trauma or loss. Maybe you find yourself stopped cold by cancer, a car accident, or the death of a loved one. Maybe it's a truck that jolts you from behind and sends you reeling. Maybe it's a lost relationship, a financial meltdown, or a long illness. Some come face-to-face with death itself. One way or another, there comes a point where you turn a corner and find you're not on solid ground anymore. You are Wile E. Coyote running along full tilt after the Road Runner and suddenly there's nothing but air beneath you as you hover for a moment then plummet to the canyon floor.

But if you are still breathing, then this is not the end of the story – far from it. After you hit bottom, what's next? The real question isn't whether we'll feel some pain in this life – we all do. The question is how we deal with it when it comes. Do we stay down when we get knocked out or can we learn how to get back up and get moving again? And if we do pick ourselves up, what's next? Can we take the big ball of trouble life threw at us and unwrap it to find the gifts hidden inside? And when we find those gifts, what form will they take? Where will they lead us?

A funny thing about a crisis that stops you in your tracks is that as hard as something like this can be, it really can be an opportunity because it leaves us primed for change. A crisis that threatens our life or blocks old paths forces us to ask questions, perhaps uncomfortable ones about who we are and where we're going. We seem to learn the most about ourselves when a crisis strips away our defenses, leaving us exposed to the raw immediacy of life. We see the world with fresh eyes when old limitations and assumptions are cleared away.

Some people struggle for years to find a place where they are free from the fears and limits they have placed on themselves. Some people never get there. Others (like Rob) have been through such a profound crisis that their slate is wiped clean, forcing them to suddenly divert their life to a dramatically new direction, to write a whole new story for themselves.

While in the hospital after his bone marrow transplant, Rob lay in a high fever for days until he finally let go and found himself standing in a misty train station, a train pulling in. His father, who had passed years before, got off the train, looked at his son, and said that they had been waiting for him. It was time to go. Rob made a choice there and then: he turned away from his father sadly and returned to fight his cancer with renewed purpose – living out the new life he'd been given, bringing gifts back from that misty station; gifts he now shares with us.

Dr. Nicole Eastman was always a driven, goal-oriented person, always looking ahead, but she never saw the truck coming that would plow into her car's rear-end, sending her into a spin and hitting her again and again. Over the next months, as she tried to recover, she felt her life falling apart, with everything for which she had worked so hard slipping away. After hitting bottom, she realized that she must have a purpose, and it was up to her to make it happen.

Mark Black was born with a heart defect and instantly rushed from the delivery room for open heart surgery while his parents anxiously awaited news of his condition. By age 23 Mark needed a heart-lung transplant, a rare and risky procedure. Just days after the surgery, still weak and with tubes in his body, he sat up in his hospital bed and decided he wasn't going to let this setback stop him. He was going to run a marathon. Since then Mark has run several races and regularly gives motivational speeches on the power of hope and strength. He has gone on to achieve far more than anyone thought possible.

After achieving her personal best in a half-marathon at age 31, **Alyssa Phillips** thought she was in the best shape of her life. All of this changed on a routine visit to her doctor when she found she had an advanced, rare, and deadly form of cervical cancer and was given a five percent chance of living through it. These odds only strengthened her resolve to keep the flame of hope alive, survive, and work to help others overcome their own challenges.

These people, and the others we meet in this book, went through difficult times, as rough as they come, but this book isn't really about that. It's about what came afterwards. Rob, Mark, Nicole, Alyssa, and others faced tremendous emotional and physical challenges, but they did not stop having hope, having strength, and having the determination to beat back whatever it was that stood in their way. They willed themselves to survive, and for all they lost, they came through it all filled with the deep knowledge that their new life was a precious gift that could not be wasted.

As amazing as survival was for these 14 people, surviving wasn't enough – they had to do more. They felt drawn to find a higher purpose with which they could connect and be a part of. And they found that the only thing that really matters at the end of the day is helping others. By connecting with others, these 14 souls tapped into a reservoir of strength that helped to heal themselves. They discovered the healing power of helping others to make their new life richer than the old life they had left behind.

This is the gift they've been given, and the gift they're giving us with their stories. We won't have the same experiences they've had – we each have our own path to follow. But we can follow the sign posts they leave, using the gifts they brought back from the edge to light our way.

Talking with Rob and the others can be a lot to absorb sometimes. To clear my mind and let it all sink in, I'll occasionally stop to go out and walk in a nearby canyon, stretching my legs. In the spring the grass grows thick on the hills and down in the canyon, and mustard plants spread splashes of yellow as Spring moves toward Summer.

Walking along, I watch a group of small birds fly up out of the grass to perch in some nearby trees. The birds speak to each other brightly, back and forth. I sit on a stone and I wonder what each of these stories means for my own life. I wonder how many other people in the world have their own story to tell, stories of passing through the fire, of seeing their old life left behind and a new brighter life unfolding before them. Stories of reaching out to each other in a world filled with both confusion and hope, full of both darkness and light. How can I use the gifts that these courageous people are offering to me? How can all of us benefit?

Come on - let's meet Rob and the others, read their stories and see where their journey leads us.

Chapter 1: Gifts from the Train Station

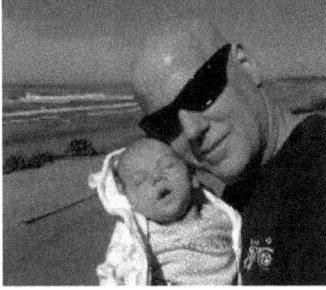

Rob Meadows grew up the third of four boys. His mother was creative and energetic; his father was solid, quiet, and engaged. As his mother struggled to find meaning in her own life, the family moved every two years from the time Rob was four on. They lived in several states and even went to New Zealand for several years. By the time he was 18, Rob had attended 12 different schools in two countries. All throughout, Maynard Meadows, Rob's father, supported his wife's wanderlust with a gentle smile and a sincere "Yes, dear."

The love between father and son was tangible and mutual. Maynard was very proud when he attended the reception where Rob received his PhD in Chemistry with a focus on Human Biochemistry. He joked that Rob had come a long way from the bottom of the class in a rural Kentucky high school to shaking the hand of the Dean of Purdue University. He bragged to strangers at the local Cracker Barrel about his son "the doctor".

Then, in 2008, the unimaginable happened. Mark, Rob's brother, was in a near-fatal car crash. He entered a vegetative coma and was not expected to live. Maynard went to the hospital every day, week after week, month after month. Mark didn't improve and the outcome became obvious. One gloomy day in November, Rob's father faced the inevitable and went to the local funeral parlor – there he made the arrangements to bury Mark, his second son.

Afterwards, Maynard went home and he told his wife, Ruth, that he wasn't hungry and just wanted to go to bed. The next morning, Rob got a tearful phone call from his mother. His father Maynard had died in his sleep.

I talked with Rob about his experiences in his office. He had popped off his favorite dog-eared leather shoes which were tucked neatly under his desk. Seated comfortably in his hand-me-down, one-armed office chair, wearing grey three-day old stubble, he looked tired but relaxed, his monitors casting a glow on his face.

Rob spoke in a low, calm voice as he told me this story, a tone that said much more than words alone could of these events from years earlier. It wasn't that his father had been ill. Rob felt that Maynard had died of a broken heart at what happened to his son.

> *"I was devastated,"* said Rob. *"There were so many things I wanted to share with him. So many things I still needed to say. I wanted to thank him for being who he was and thank him for teaching me how to be who I am. I miss him every day and regret not taking the time to tell him how important he really was in my life. I thought it odd at the time, but Ruth told me that he went peacefully and had a smile on his face when she found him."*

> *"At the time, like all of us, I swore to make every day count; that I wouldn't just survive, but I would live and make my father proud. But, like most of us, reality set in: traffic, bills, grocery shopping, work, and all of life's other mundane events crept back into and overtook my life. In a few months, the feeling of urgency to live every day had faded."*

Then, I could see in Rob's eyes the movement forward through the years, and his face brightens as he shifts in his chair and talks about his wife.

> *"Although she is much smarter than me, my wife Vicki and I are of similar scientific backgrounds. We had both been working hard in the pharmaceutical industry in San Diego doing drug discovery, trying to find cures for devastating illnesses like cancer. We had met in the 1990s, she was the girlfriend of one of my lab mates, but over time, she came around. We were married on April 9th, 2007 and settled into a comfortable life, working, dreaming of the future, and raising her two wonderful children."*

In the spring of 2009, Vicki and Rob went on a trip to Tuscany. I had known Rob for several years and this was the first time that I could remember him taking any time off. It was unusual, but it looked like he needed it. He'd always looked young for his age, but those days, in early 2009, he just looked tired.

> *"The Tuscan countryside was gorgeous and the people were warm and inviting. Two months after we returned, we learned that Vicki was pregnant. This was quite a surprise since I was 51 and Vicki was 45 and a few years earlier she had significant surgery that left her with only one ovary. We were amazed, bewildered, grateful and ecstatic that our little miracle baby was on the way. All of the tests showed that she was healthy and she was due to arrive on December 1st of that year."*

As the year progressed, Rob started running a low grade fever with a small but constant sniffle. He told me that he felt tired all the time and, typical for Rob, he laughed it off by saying that he was getting old and the transition from one year to the next simply was not as smooth as when we were young men.

Rob continued…

"These nagging little symptoms persisted so I went to the doctor who prescribed antibiotics. A few weeks later, after it was clear that the antibiotics weren't working, we tried two or three rounds of more aggressive therapies. Nothing seemed to work but I kept going back, afraid I would pass on an infection to my wife and unborn baby. We kept at this until September, when the doctor finally did some blood work. The results came back in a week and they looked awful. When I went back to the doctor he then recommended a GI specialist and an oncologist. I was confused – why would I need an oncologist for a sniffle?"

In late November, he finally got in to see the two specialists. The GI doctor found nothing, but the oncologist looked him dead in the eye and said, "Get on the table. I'm going to do a bone marrow biopsy."

"I immediately hesitated, I had heard that a bone marrow biopsy was one of the most uncomfortable and invasive procedures still in use today. Regardless, I sighed, turned white, and got on the table. I have to say candidly that had I not been married with a baby on the way, I would not have done it. I would have walked out. And I would be dead now."

On December 1st, just as predicted, Abigail Victoria Meadows was born. She was a 6lbs 4oz beautiful baby girl.

"I was on top of the world. Fifteen days later, December 16th, on a clear, warm San Diego day, I was in a chair in our bedroom, my back warmed by the sun, watching the beauty of my wife Vicki breastfeeding our miracle baby. Abby's tiny feet were in the air and she was purring."

"It was a perfect moment, one of the few that I have had in my life."

"And then the phone rang. It was my doctor."

"He asked me three questions:

'Are you at home'

'Are you with family?'

'Are you sitting down?'

"The rest of the conversation was him telling me that I had an advanced case of Acute Myelogenous Leukemia and that my prognosis was that I had maybe two months to live. That was 3:30, and by 6 PM I was in a hospital bed being prepped for chemotherapy."

As the reader may recall, that was the winter of the swine flu scare. Hospitals were very strict about who they let in. Children, older adults, the unwell were all banned from visiting their loved ones. It was also Christmas time – caroling, celebration of family and faith, chestnuts roasting on an open fire.

"Abby was not allowed in the hospital, and so I spent the next 32 days alone, crying when the nurses sang Christmas carols, questioning everything, including faith and God, and battling for my life."

This was the first of four rounds of chemotherapy for Rob. And, along the way, tests verified that his particular cytogenetic profile and mutations were aggressive and the cancer would likely come back – chemotherapy was just going to put things off for a year or two. The only hope for a cure was a bone marrow transplant.

"So we began testing my surviving siblings in the hopes of finding for immunological match. Statistics show that more than 70% of patients can not find suitable donors in their

family. That was my case. So, unfortunately, both brothers were far from ideal matches. My last hope was to find a generous person somewhere in the world that was a good match and still alive and healthy. So the National Bone Marrow Registry looked into the international database and found two perfect matches, both in the UK. They were 10 out of 10 on the testing scales. This, along with Abigail's arrival, was yet another miracle."

"On May 15th, 2010, I received a stem-cell based bone marrow transplant. I know there is a lot of controversy about stem cells, but as I learned, there are many, many different kinds of stem cells. The kinds that I received are like blood cells: they look like blood cells and are collected at facilities like the Red Cross, blood banks and blood drives. These cells circulate in the blood in all of us. My donor was a male, in his late 20's, living in Europe. He got a call that he could save someone's life, went to his local hospital and donated about a pint of stem cells that were collected directly from his blood. The cells were couriered across the Atlantic and on to San Diego."

"The nurses hung the little bag of red cells and told me that this was my second birthday," he said. *Rob's life started again, that day."*

The transplant was a life saver, but it was just the start. Stem cell transplants are not an easy solution, and Rob still had many hurdles to get over, some of them very high. The survival rate for stem cell transplants is about 50/50. The job of our immune system is to attack anything from somewhere else, including what is essentially a new body, like Rob's.

"Two weeks after receiving the stem cells, I started running a temperature. This new European immune system was attacking my body. At first the fever was 100° F, and then it went up to 102°, 104°, and finally I stabilized with a raging fever of about 106°."

"It went on for days. I was packed in ice and given cold showers, but still the fever went on and on. As soon as any blood product effused my new bone marrow, it was burned up – incinerated by the heat. Especially critical were the platelets. Platelets allow blood to clot and normally have values of 120,000-400,000. I had 4,000. A bump on the head would have killed me. They could not infuse me with platelets with a fever over 102° – it was pointless. I waited, burning like a rocket, dying."

"It was on the third day or so of the fever that I started feeling very comfortable, very relaxed, and I felt as if I was melting into the bed and fading from this life. I wanted to let go. I was so tired of fighting and putting on a strong face for my family. I didn't even know if it was worth it. What if I struggled and struggled and it was all for nothing? I let go. I released myself from the responsibility of fighting."

Rob closed his eyes and his breathing slowed as he relaxed into his chair. He was quiet for a moment before speaking again slowly and quietly…

"I don't know how long it took, a few hours maybe, but it was then that I started seeing the white light. I say seeing, but it wasn't really that. And it wasn't a light in the Thomas Edison light bulb sense. And it wasn't coming from somewhere outside of me or shining into my face. It was coming from within me. I know it. It was real. It felt as if it was my spirit

*leaving my body. It was the lord taking me. It was the God
that lives inside each and every one of us that was leaving
me."*

Rob hesitated and looked distantly out the window, tapping his thigh nervously with his right index finger as he rocked back and forth gently. As he turned his face away from me, I could see that this conversation, this memory, had real significance for him. It went deep, the kind of deep we don't often share with others, even friends and family. He breathed deeply for a few seconds, looked down at his arms, which, because of residual graft-versus-host, are an indicator of his emotional state. He shook them out, took another breath and continued slowly, almost whispering.

*"I opened my eyes and I could see only the light. Everything
else started to fade. I closed my eyes and the light filled
everything and warmed and comforted me. It was
unavoidable, brilliant and inviting."*

*"As the light dimmed, I realized that I was at a steamy train
station. The train was sitting, breathing white mist, waiting for
passengers. And out from the train came my father,
Maynard. It was the man that I had missed so much, every
day, and whose passing had left such a void in my life and
soul. He had a concerned look on his face. I have seen that
look many times when he wanted to tell me something that I
didn't want to hear, or get me to do something that he knew I
wouldn't like. He came up to me and said, 'Hey Buddy. We
have your room ready. It's time to go. It's time to get on the
train.' He held out his arm to bring me in."*

*"I so wanted to go. I miss him every day. I never got to say
goodbye or any of the things a grown man should say to his*

> *father. God could not have picked a better emissary to guide me to my next destination."*

Rob sighed and looked back at me, then down at his feet, looking right through the carpet and the floor. I looked down at the floor next to his feet as well, at the cords snaking under his desk, pretty sure I was not seeing the same thing as Rob at this moment.

> *"I looked down. I was on the passenger side of the station and the train was on the track side. I saw the little gap in the concrete that separated us and I couldn't cross it. I couldn't lift my foot and step over that crack, I couldn't cross that threshold. I had a baby girl that needed me. I had a wife that needed me. I have work to do. I need to find decent drugs for childhood cancers and illnesses of the elderly. I need to give to the needy and teach and support. There was still so much to do. I have so much unfinished business, both with my life's work and with the people I love."*

> *"So, I gave my dad a sad smile, and shook my head. I turned away. It was the hardest thing I have ever done."*

Rob looked up at me and he was back: his eyes were sad, tear-filled, and the corners of his mouth were drawn tight.

> *"When the light faded, I could see my wife and she was screaming at me, 'Don't go. Don't leave us. We need you.'*

> *"I came back. I have spent many months recovering from the illness and the transplant, and the recovery is still continuing as the graft-versus-host flares up from time to time. I have watched Abby grow and take her first steps, and I have returned to work as my health has improved. But things are not the same. The experiences I went through have not gone away or even faded. When I close my eyes, I can still feel the*

> train there in front of me in the mist, and I can see my father reaching out."

Rob stops and shivers slightly, even with long sleeves and the heater running.

> "Things have changed for good, I think. The last couple of years have been hard for me in many ways, and hard for my family. I'm pretty sure I would not be volunteering for this experience or anything like it. But having lived it, and survived it, I can look forward knowing there's a new life ahead for me, a life different than the one I was headed for before. I did not truly appreciate before all that God has given me in life. I really did have a new birthday in the hospital that day, and on every day since then."

Rob sits up, and I sit up too, the pace of his voice quickening as I struggle to keep up with my notes, listening raptly, afraid to miss a word.

> "On that day I realized many things," he began.

> "Every day from thereafter was a gift. God let me come back. He truly is merciful. I'm still recovering from the transplant, and dealing with immunosuppressant drugs and graft-versus-host disease – some days are hard, but I wake each day grateful to be here, and ready to make the most of it."

> "I realized that I am not afraid to die. I have been to the edge of life and I had a glimpse of what lays beyond. It is warm and comforting. There is nothing to fear anymore. I don't know what is beyond the station, but it doesn't matter anymore. The important thing is that I am here for now, and that is more than enough."

"And I also learned that it is so true that you leave this world with nothing. Things, money, status are all completely meaningless at our next destination. The house that you live in will be owned by someone else. They will repaint, remodel, and redo all of the things that were about you. They won't care about you or know you. Your car will be driven by a stranger – perhaps way too fast for your liking, or they will lower it, shred it, and Fast and Furious it. And your money, well, it goes wherever money goes."

"I realized that what we leave behind, for most of us anyway, are not the results of our work, the records of our accomplishments, or our little trophies and medals. What most of us leave behind that will live on after us, are simply memories. And they are not our memories, not the ones in our heads – those fade with us. Our legacy is the memories that we leave with other people. Like the memory of that summer at the lake house when we taught Richie how to fish. He will still have that memory long after I'm gone. Like the memory that the scout troop has from when they received a large donation from a stranger that enabled them to compete in Australia at the International Scouting Jamboree. Those kids will have memories enabled by a gift from a stranger. Vicki will remember our last kiss for the rest of her life. And Abby will remember that her Daddy called a glass of water "glug glug." I hope it will make her smile."

"I realized that giving is not an option, it is an imperative. If there is anything I can do to make the lives of people and families easier, then I need to do it. It has to be done here. It has to be done now."

"I realized that everyone has a story. You might not like someone, you may hate them, they may have done you

wrong, but they are still a creation of God and they have known joy and heartache, they have dreams and hopes, and they have suffered failures and hardships. They have a life story and it is just as important as yours."

"I realized that family is as important as food. Abigail saved my life. Vicki saved my life. Ruth, Pat and Patti, Peggy and Greg, and the rest of the Glenns, who are my extended family, helped save my life."

"I realized that thoughts and prayers are real. They get to where they need to go. Sometimes, tragically, they are simply not enough. But sometimes, as for me, they helped tip the balance. I could feel them pulling me back from the train station."

'You're not ready.'

'Please come home to us.'

'We want you to be healthy and happy again.'

"They all helped me. And I, and my family, we're forever grateful."

By the time Rob is done talking, I'm the one with shivers. We finish up, comparing notes about a few things, and I walk out, thinking about my own life. I've never been through anything even remotely like what Rob has experienced, but somehow even just hearing him makes me feel like I have a new lease on life as well, with far more to do. It is as if some of his glow has rubbed off on me, and stays with me as I leave his office and go back to the rest of my day. If I feel that I have too much to do and wonder how I can deal with it, all I have to do is think of Rob. Rob got this all started, sending me down the road that led to meeting and talking with all the others in this book, and thinking about what it all means. I'm hoping this book is a way to carry forward this hope and excitement at the opportunities life offers us, some of them disguised as problems. I hope some of this rubs off on you as well and those around you, spreading outward like ripples from a stone thrown into a pond.

Rob continues his good work today, reaching out to tell his story to others who find themselves in challenging times. He works occasionally with the National Leukemia and Lymphoma Society. At the website below, you can find more about Rob and other people like him who are building a life reaching out to help others.

The only thing that matters at the end of the day is the help that we give to each other.

Find out more and get involved at: www.giftsfromthetrainstation.com

Chapter 2: Transaplant Survivor and Thriver

Mark Black was born in Canada with aortic stenosis, a defect in the aortic valve of the heart that prevented blood from reaching the rest of his body. As soon as he was born, his skin turned blue and the doctors rushed him out of the room, telling his nervous parents that their baby boy needed open-heart surgery right away. He was put in an incubator and flown immediately via helicopter for surgery while his parents waited, uncertain of their baby's future.

Mark had two open-heart surgeries before his first birthday. His heart condition, while less acute, was still there through his childhood and checked periodically by his doctors. Thinking back, his heart problem never held him back much in his childhood, not at first at least; he didn't realize that what was normal for him wasn't normal for everyone else.

> *"The majority of the time when I was growing up my heart problem wasn't a big issue,"* said Mark. *"I had never known anything different, so things like having a scar or going to visit cardiologists seemed normal to me. I think I was six before I realized that other kids didn't have a big scar down the middle of their chest."*

Over the years his condition slowly deteriorated, and by the time he was 23 years old something had to be done, and quickly. He was told by his doctors that he would die within two years unless he received a heart-lung transplant, and the odds for a successful heart-lung transplant were not good, with few of these rare and risky surgeries conducted every year.

Getting on the transplant list in October 2001 was a big step forward for Mark, but only the first step. He still had to wait for the right donor, and had to be near the transplant center at all times, ready to go at a moment's notice.

> *"I moved with my dad 1,000 miles away from my home and the rest of our family, to Toronto, Ontario where they could perform the surgery. I was given a pager and told not to go outside a 150 mile radius of the hospital so that when the pager went off, I would be ready. I couldn't afford to miss the call – there might not be another chance."*

Days passed, and then weeks, and then months, waiting for the pager to go off that would tell the Blacks that a donor had been found. Fall turned to winter, and Christmas came and went with Mark still waiting far from home. Meanwhile, his heart grew worse and he had to stay in the hospital around the clock, confined to a small room where he was constantly monitored, living there for six months while he read and spent time with his family. Starting a journal and writing in it every day also helped him deal with the brewing anxiety that came with the waiting.

> *"The journal writing helped me process my fears and feelings, and also motivated me to write my book after the transplant, looking forward."*

Then one day it finally happened: the call came. While waiting in his hospital room Mark was told that there was a call for him at the nurse station. "Mr. Black, I think we have a heart and lungs for you," the woman on the phone said to Mark.

Imagine the moment. After so much time, the wait was finally over. Mark and his family might have worried more when the call finally came, thinking through everything that might go wrong, but there was little time for worrying. The surgery had to happen quickly after the donor organs were identified, within hours.

> *"There wasn't a lot of time to think or feel anything,"* said Mark. *"But in that time I was mostly excited. Of course there were nerves, but I wasn't really scared. I was going to die without the transplant. I knew that for sure, so I had nothing to lose. As a result I was much calmer than I expected I'd be."*

The staff came at 5 AM to take Mark to the operating room. Mark looked at his mom, thinking briefly about the full range of possibilities that the future might hold. There were so many things they could say, in case it did not work out, but he decided not to talk about his fears.

> *"All I could say was, 'Mom, I'm going to see you soon.'"*

Mark had the transplant surgery on September 7th, 2002, and quickly started the long recovery process, moving forward step by step and never looking back.

> *"I was in surgery for 7 hours, followed by many days, weeks, and months of arduous recovery,"* he said.

First came the ICU, with Mark on a ventilator for the first few days. Then he spent another ten days on the transplant floor, which is kept scrupulously clean to avoid infection in vulnerable transplant patients who are on immunosuppressant drugs to prevent their body from rejecting their new organs. Even after being discharged, Mark had to return as an outpatient almost every day for ongoing tests, x-rays, and physical therapy, often showing up at 6 AM and spending the whole day at the hospital.

The physical challenges were great, and Mark still takes immunosuppressants every day, leaving him vulnerable to infections. But the mental challenges can be even greater.

> *"As hard as this was physically, and it was exhausting when I was still recovering from surgery, the mental side was tougher,"* said Mark. *"Often the progress was slow and there were many hiccups along the way, like the steroid-induced depression that sometimes made even getting out of bed a challenge. I got through it with the help of God, my family, and an attitude that there was something worth all of the work on the other side of that challenge."*

Early on the path to recovery, Mark made a decision. He decided that surviving wasn't enough. Surviving is a great thing and something to celebrate, but he knew that if he stopped with survival and didn't strive for more, then he was missing out on this chance that had been given to him. He'd been near death, and had been given another chance to live. The past was gone, and a new unwritten future lay ahead, waiting for him to write it. He committed to himself that he was going to do more with his life, more than anyone thought he could. He was in it for the long run, and there was no better way to show the world how far he could go than to get up out of his bed after the heart-lung transplant and start running.

It had been years at the time since Mark had run at all, much less over any kind of distance. But he felt deep within that he had to do it. Rather than worry about all the reasons why it was hard or why it might not make sense, he committed himself to doing it and then figured out how to make it happen.

> *"Just seven days after the surgery, I sat up in the hospital bed and decided I was going to run a marathon. I weighed 80 pounds at the time, had been trapped indoors for ages, and*

had various tubes and wires inserted into my body to make sure things were coming along well. I was never the fastest, but I had run cross country as a kid. I was, and still am, very small, so the shorter distances were never for me. I preferred to run long. I knew the longer the race, the more big guys I could catch. For me to talk about running a marathon after the surgery must have sounded crazy to people at the time. People told me that if everything worked well and I was lucky I might, just might, be able to go back to work part-time. But I had decided, and that was all it took. The process was started."

Maybe taking a big step like this, setting a goal others may have viewed as crazy at the time, helped Mark to prove he could do anything, that his life was not limited by his heart or by anything else.

"It scares me what my life would be if I let those expectations shape my life. I could not listen to those who had low expectations."

Realizing his dream meant hard work, and a lot of it, he began with physical therapy, then stepped up to a treadmill. From there he accomplished a 5K and a 10K, then his first half-marathon for his 26th birthday. Two and a half years later he ran his first marathon.

And it all started with that simple commitment in his hospital bed, and letting absolutely nothing stand in his way.

Today, Mark travels all over North America talking to businesses, schools, and other groups about what he learned while overcoming his life's challenges, and people respond, connecting strongly with him because of the great challenges they face in their own lives. And four marathons, a marriage, two kids, one book, and countless talks later, Mark's story is still far from over. He works for his family, and for the people he meets, sharing the hard-won lessons he earned. What worked for him, and still helps him now, can work for any of us.

Mark gathered four key lessons that he shares in his book "*Living Life from the Heart*" and in his talks. These are the lessons that kept him going in his hospital bed, keep him going in a long grueling marathon, and keep him going today, continuing to strive to make the most of the second chance he's been given.

1. Accentuate the Positive. *"Every day many, many times we decide how we are going to handle things. We can decide to focus on the positive, or not. By deciding to focus on the positive, you move your life in a positive direction."*

2. Live Today. *"Many of us will waste big chunks of our life worrying about things we have absolutely no control over at all. I could spend each day worrying, but I made a commitment to live this day the best I can."*

3. Go Big. *"Ask yourself if your goals are big enough. The purpose of goals is to push your vision, to stretch and push yourself out of your comfort zone. Setting high goals means doing more than we thought we could, achieving big things."*

4. Refuse to Quit. *"No matter how hard things get, no matter what happens and whatever you think, never believe that you won't make it. Never give up. Refuse to quit. If you do this one thing, you cannot fail."*

It's amazing how far Mark has gone after facing down death, reaching out to people everywhere. I picture him in that hospital bed after his transplant surgery at the moment when he decided he was headed for a much larger future. He might not have known all that would come in the years ahead, but he knew that no matter where he was at that moment, he could and would do great things. He showed me that we each hold our future in our own hands. It's a big lesson, and one that I keep learning over and over again, with the help of people like Mark.

Get in contact with Mark to learn more or book him as a speaker at: Mark@MarkBlackSpeaks.com

Mark's book "*Living Life from the Heart*" is available on Amazon, or on Mark's website at www.MarkBlackSpeaks.com, telling Mark's whole incredible story and helping others to learn from his experiences.

Chapter 3: Reaching a New Life

Many of us have the nagging feeling that we should be doing more with our lives, that we have a calling that we missed along the way somehow, a passion we abandoned or never connected with. It's like we missed our turnoff from the freeway and end up lost, far down the road, with no idea how we got there. Maybe we're afraid that our dream isn't practical, that it is too risky, or that we might fall flat on our face and fail. Some end their lives still regretting, still wishing they had released their fears and given their dreams a chance.

Alice Chan was one of these people who felt something crucial was absent from her life. Alice was a success by most measures, with a nice home in the San Francisco Bay Area, a good job in market research consulting, and a healthy salary. Some would wonder what else you could ask for, but Alice wasn't happy. While her life looked like the picture of success to others, it felt empty to her. By 2008, she was deeply unhappy and did not know where to turn. Her career seemed a hollow victory, and she felt herself lost and wandering. Seeking the answers in an avalanche of self-help books and courses, she was soon more confused than ever.

> *"I got into the market research and business consulting world when I left my academic career and moved out to the Bay Area in 2001,"* said Alice. *"I was teaching and doing research in new media at Cornell University, and I joined a firm that specialized in the IT sector. Over time, though, I found that*

> *the work wasn't personally meaningful. I was, and I still am, more interested in human development."*

> *"I had long since outgrown my job at the time. At a deeper level, I had hated myself for years for having 'sold out' by becoming a business consultant, as it didn't match my psychological picture of being a helper in this life. It wasn't personally meaningful work to me. In addition to being in crisis, I was also overwhelmed by the vast amount of self-help tools out there."*

We often struggle to reach a point where we feel we will finally have the money, position, and status to be happy. Often we never get there, no matter how hard we work or how far we go. Even as we progress and make more, it never seems enough to fill the void within. Money and status are not the answer if we don't have a purpose in our lives that allows us to contribute to something larger than ourselves.

When a friend invited Alice to Sedona in 2008, she went seeking insight and finally found it. She realized on that trip that she was not alone, and that many others like her go through the same search for purpose, the same difficulty in making the move toward a new and better life. She envisioned a solution: REACH, a book and workshops she would create showing people how to find their own inner purpose and pursue it, living the full, rich lives they had always dreamt of – lives filled with meaning. By doing this, she would be aligned with the true purpose of her own life as well.

> *"Then it hit me, in a very intuitive way, that it was my job to create an integrated system to help others who experience similar pain as I did. That was when the concept of REACH came to me effortlessly. I was supposed to write a book and teach this program to others."*

Alice saw what she needed to do, and yet had difficulty getting started. Sometimes, even when the new path becomes clear to us, it can be hard to embark on it, to let go of all that we have known and further, set out into the unknown. It's normal, it's human, and these contemplations live deep inside each of us. Self-preservation and a quest for safety have been embedded in us since humans started to walk upright, sometimes driving us to stick to the safe path even if we know it's not the best path.

> *"I was afraid, and didn't feel qualified to be the messenger of REACH. Nobody knew who I was; how was I going to make it work? So, I reverted right back to doing the job I hated and had outgrown but was very good at, because it was safe."*

Sometimes the universe makes the decision for us. For Alice, a car accident at the end of 2008 made the decision to change her life much easier as old fears faded away.

> *"Then I was in a near-fatal car accident on December 30th, 2008. While still unconscious in the hospital, before I knew what had happened to me, I had a 'God experience' that told me I almost died, but was kept alive because there was more for me to do in this life. I was wrapped up from head to toe in a warm cocoon of the purest love that's unlike any human experience. I didn't feel any fear with knowing that I almost died; everything was well and in right order."*

As we shall see in subsequent chapters, when an accident like this happens, people face a fork in the road. One direction leads to feeling sorry for yourself: you have had such a trauma and been through such difficulty. The other path leads in a completely different direction: rethinking things and committing to making the most of life, regardless of the problems you have and maybe even because of them. It can be hard to see it this way, but the accident or other problem is often an opportunity to start anew. It gives an opportunity to rewrite our story, to create a new story for who we are and where we are headed.

> *"My time wasn't up yet, because there was more for me to do in this life. And I wasn't going to live out my second lease in life continuing to mark time as I did prior to the accident. I needed to fulfill my life purpose."*

> *"The experience of being held by divine love and knowing that all was well and in right order (even though my human self was unconscious and hooked up to all kinds of machines) is a big part of what keeps me going, reminding me why I'm still alive."*

> *"I have no memory of the accident, because I lost consciousness and suffered some memory loss. The neurosurgeon also said that I'll probably never remember the incident because of how traumatic it was. I was in a high-speed collision on a freeway – my head was really banged up. I woke up three days later with staples running across my head and an open wound on the left side of my head."*

> *"Recovering was difficult. It took me more than half a year to regain enough physical strength to feel normal again. During that time, I also felt scared and alone – symptoms of post-traumatic stress. For more than a year, I dealt with dizziness every night when I laid down to go to sleep and every morning when I tried to get out of bed. I still deal with occasional dizziness now."*

The physical recovery was difficult for Alice, but the real recovery began when she launched her new life with her new purpose: building her REACH program to help others.

"I work to help others now through workshops/seminars and coaching, based on the 5-step personal empowerment program in my book, "REACH Your Dreams: Five Steps to be a Conscious Creator in Your Life". For instance, I led a workshop this morning with a group of women entrepreneurs in the San Francisco Bay Area. I'll be doing teleseminars starting in mid-December going through mid-January to help participants release the old (i.e., forgotten limiting beliefs), envision for the new year, and activate the new by taking action in an inspired, purposeful way."

"The accident happened to wake me up to getting on with why I'm here in this life. I couldn't hide in my comfort zone anymore."

The lessons Alice gained from her experience that have led her forward are:

1. There's a greater purpose. My soul took on this physical body to fulfill my purpose in this life.

2. My job is to keep saying "yes" to the next step that is calling me towards fulfilling it, no matter how irrational it may seem at face value.

3. As long as I keep up with lesson #2, the universe will never leave me stranded, but instead line up what I need to fulfill my purpose.

4. Living without purpose, marking time in this life, will never be an option again.

It's not easy to change. Few of us would choose to leave our comfort zone, even if we're unhappy in it, without feeling enough pain or upheaval. Where there is the will, there is always a way, though. If someone chooses to change their life, they always can.

There are many people in the world who look successful but don't feel successful, feeling that their hard-won success is a hollow victory if it lacks a connection to a greater purpose. At first glance, it can be hard to understand how someone like Alice can walk away from a successful career straight into pure uncertainty, until you see how important having a greater purpose is. When it's time to lay your cards on the table and see what you've done with your life, reaching out to help others seems to count for far more than fame and wealth. People like Alice show us how we don't have to wait for the end to realize this, nor do we need to court a near-death experience to wake up to a greater purpose to be served by us in this life. The truth is here and now, awaiting those who are ready to see it.

Alice works to live up this potential for herself, and for those she works with:

We all have a greater purpose – look within yourself to let it unfold.

Keep moving forward, even if it takes you in unexpected directions; take chances that your gut says are yours to take.

Unwaveringly move towards your goals, no matter how many times you get discouraged. Never give up.

Always live with purpose, as you'll be far happier than if you just mark time.

Alice Chan offers seminars, workshops, and coaching programs, and can be reached through her website. How to contact: www.dralicechan.com

Chapter 4: Running for Your Life

Obesity is one of the biggest health challenges of our time, with a third of US adults now obese and other parts of the world quickly following down the same path as they learn the same bad habits and suffer the same health consequences.   The reasons for this dramatic shift are not hard to see: we're eating more, eating bad food, and spending more time sitting at school, at work, and in our car. And when we get home, we sit there too. The solutions seem harder to find though. We all know that changing diet and exercise holds the answer, but making these changes stick over the long run often seems hard. **Roger Wright** of Needham, Massachusetts found an answer though that helped him to take back control of his health with diet and exercise, radically transforming his life.

Roger had struggled with obesity since he was a child, gaining weight year after year, rising to 200 pounds, 250 pounds, 300 pounds and even higher, eventually reaching 320 pounds. Year after year he would make a New Year's resolution: to lose weight, he would sign up for a gym and go a few times, but then he'd stop.

> *"I joined health clubs like an annual rite,"* he said, *"but I always had to join a new one because I couldn't show my face at the old one. After going a few times I'd stop. I was lazy. I did not like to work out because it hurt." Gaining weight was pretty easy, but losing weight unfortunately was not."*

> *"I loved to eat, and I loved to eat bad food. Bad food tastes good. Everybody loves pizza."*

Roger tried diets – lots of them. They would work at first, but none of them did enough, and he'd lose five or ten pounds then celebrate and put the weight back on. He knew it was a problem, but had plenty of reasons in his mind as to why he could not follow through.

Wright is easy to talk with; he's a genuinely nice guy who speaks openly about being overweight, which is not always easy. We often avoid the subject with obese friends or family who we are afraid of offending. Once, on a flight to Las Vegas with his brother, Roger realized that his seat belt wouldn't snap closed. He was deeply embarrassed. He tried to hide the open seat belt with his jacket in his lap, but the stewardess came and he had to say the belt would not close. The stewardess left and returned with a seat belt extender they had on hand for just this reason.

> *"She apologized, saying the seat belt was shorter than the others, that they really had to get it fixed,"* said Roger. *"But I knew it was the same, that she was being kind. My brother turned to me and said, 'Dude, you've got to lose weight.' I told myself I was going to change. But I stole the extender and used it for the next 3-4 years so I would not have to ask for it again."*

Even after difficult moments like this, Roger did not really lose weight until June 2008, when certain events propelled Roger to make a real change in his life, a lasting shift to get healthy and stay healthy.

One thing to occur that year was that his niece with cystic fibrosis, Julia, was put on a transplant list for her lungs, and she was not doing well. Cystic fibrosis is a genetic disease that affects about 30,000 people in the US, making breathing difficult as well as causing other health issues. While treatment for CF patients has improved over the years, there is still no cure.

In addition to hearing the news about his niece, Roger watched the Boston Marathon that April, remembering his dream of running it one day. Then his doctor told him that he was now borderline diabetic, with his cholesterol through the roof. He was at 300 pounds, and remembered that he had made a resolution to go on the TV show The Biggest Loser. After spending hours filling out the lengthy application, he found that it was too late, that the show had already started filming for the season. He had missed his opportunity, he told himself, and his mind went to work searching the reasons why. The next thing he knew he found himself outside grilling ribs, telling himself that he needed to gain still more weight, to be even more obese in order to make it on the next season of the Biggest Loser.

Sometimes people have to hit bottom before they bounce back and set out in a new direction. This was Roger's rock bottom moment, grilling the ribs, but in the next moment the answer came to him in a flash.

> *"There I was, standing there grilling the ribs, two racks for myself, and it all came together,"* said Roger.

It was time. He'd come to the end of one road, but the new road ahead came to him, all the pieces coming together. He did not need the Biggest Loser to lose weight, he realized. If he really wanted to lose the weight, he could do it without the show, but not just for himself. He would do it for Julia, for his family, and to show obese people everywhere that they could do it too.

Roger came in from the grill and told his wife -

> *"I'm going to train, lose 50 pounds, run the Boston Marathon, and raise money for Julia for cystic fibrosis."*

His wife could have said anything. She could have easily been skeptical after years of his failed diets and health clubs, but she wasn't. She must have seen in his eyes that this was real, and she must have known how important this was for all of them. His wife told him, "I think that's a great idea," giving him her total support.

> *"She said that if I ran the race she'd make sure I had a friend at every mile,"* Roger recalled. *"She was worried about me, and I was committed to her. I said to myself, 'For the first time in my life I'm going to commit myself to a change'. And I did."*

One of the first steps to follow through on his commitment was signing up for the Boston Marathon – but not just anybody can sign up. Due to its popularity, the Boston Marathon is one of the few marathons that require runners to qualify for it; fortunately, they allow 5% of the runners into the marathon on the condition that they intend to raise money for various charities.

> *"I contacted the CFF (Cystic Fibrosis Foundation) and asked them if they would be willing to obtain a number for me. They agreed; however, they required me to complete a form guaranteeing them at least $3,000 in donations. To back that up they even required my credit card information. Two minutes after receiving the form, I completed the application and sent it back. Essentially I'd forced myself to commit to this goal."*

> *"I just saw how my life was falling away,"* Roger said. He knew that if he didn't dramatically change his life, the result would not be good. *"I didn't want to go quietly into the ground. I want people to remember me in a good light, making a positive difference in the world. I hope I'm helping*

to inspire others. I committed to make my wife proud, and to make my mom proud, even though I never knew her – she died when I was just one. Making this commitment and the commitment to my niece, it just clicked. If I had not changed there's a good chance I would not be alive."

Roger started running, slowly at first but sticking with it every day and ramping up. In the first couple of weeks he saw little happen: he was losing only a few pounds even while completely changing his diet and working out far more than ever before in his life. He got mad but kept going, thinking of those around him and his commitment to them. By the one month mark a radical transformation started to take place, as revealed by pictures you can find on his website. The weight melted from his body until he hardly looked like the same person, transformed from 276 pounds to a fit and lean 163 pounds in just ten months.

Roger ran the Boston marathon for the first time in 2009 after getting himself in shape, running the whole race non-stop in 4 hours and 45 minutes. He continues to run on a daily basis, always thinking about the next race. He never stops now because for him the running is not a burden but a gift. He is running for his life and for others, always thinking of how he can inspire and help others as well as stay healthy himself. The fight against obesity and against cystic fibrosis doesn't end at the close of a race.

"There's always the next day, the next month, and the next year. I'm always running marathons, one after another. I need to have that goal that I keep in front of me, because I have a race coming up; a goal to break, to think about how I can inspire other people."

The memory of his past self is still clear in his mind, like the pictures on his website, all reminders of the danger that lurks in places like the local pizza joint. His diet is far healthier than before, although he tries not to be too rigid about it either. He eats a healthy balanced diet, but if on occasion he splurges, he doesn't beat himself up over it. He just goes back to work the next day, getting back on track again, in the race for the long run.

> *"A huge fear of mine is putting the weight back on, but I still like food. Tonight I'll go out and live life and eat, and tomorrow it'll be sardines and a banana."*

And as big a change as his weight has experienced, the bigger change is what has happened inside, as he has continued striving to help other people as well.

> *"I really just want to help people," said Roger. "That's the biggest change about me as a person."*

It might sound like a platitude coming from some people, but somehow coming from Roger it's not. It's just the simple truth. After all of the years fighting with his weight, things clicked finally and set him on a new path, one leading to true success. Making this commitment to help others, Roger changed his own life as well. I'm not sure about all of the diets and exercise plans that come out every day, but I am certain of the power of people like Roger to change their lives for the better. If there's a take home message from Roger's story, that's it: by committing ourselves to a purpose greater than ourselves, we unlock our full potential to change and heal our own lives as well.

To help Roger, you can make a donation at his site for CF, sponsoring him in one of his upcoming races. Roger also has lots of information on his site about how he achieved his personal transformation. There's no magic involved, other than the magic of the human heart and mind, and there's no reason why you can't replicate his magic in your own life no matter what challenge you face, and build a better future for yourself and others as well.

How   to   contact   Roger: www.runningformyexistence.com (www.RFME.org)

Chapter 5: Losing Everything and Gaining More

All of her life, **Dr. Nicole Eastman** was driven to succeed in everything she did, letting nothing stand in her way. She was very much a Type A personality: in control, never stopping and always pushing herself to do more. She worked up to 80 hours per week while squeezing in workouts, studying, household chores, and spending time with family and friends. Living a healthy lifestyle was important to her. Her father died of a stroke at the age of 53; with a family history of heart disease, health risks and lifestyle factors contributing to the stroke. When her father died, it only drove her to work even harder.

Unfortunately, not everything was in her control. When a truck rammed into her car, it set in motion a chain of events that took away her old life but led to a new life she never expected.

"On December 15th, 2010, my car was hit three times on the expressway by a semi truck going 65 miles per hour. I had just been married two weeks earlier and I was at the start of my career as a physician. Two days earlier there had been a severe snow storm in Michigan, but on this day the roads were clear. I was in the far right-hand lane and only two exits away from getting off of the expressway, at I-696 East near the Van Dyke exit, when the semi truck hit the back end of my car. My back took the initial impact of the large semi-truck driving between 60-65 mph. I never saw it coming and had no time to react when he hit me from behind in the left rear of

44

the car, sending my car spinning. The truck hit me again on the driver's side rear door and my car continued to spin as I lost consciousness and went under the trailer of the truck."

"I remember feeling like time was standing still. I braced for the final impact, my teeth clenching down hard, and I just kept thinking, 'I'm going to die, I'm going to die. While I braced for the final impact, I thought about the patients who I had seen in the past who were affected by brain and spinal cord injuries, and I hoped I would not be one of them. I prayed to God that He would save me."

"I guess it worked. The final impact didn't come. My car came to a stop and I found myself facing oncoming traffic, the first two right hand lanes blocked by the truck, with cars coming at me head on and swerving around me but not stopping. I still can't understand why people were driving past me and not even stopping."

"I was in a state of shock. I didn't know it at the time, but I had a mild concussion and was disoriented. I pushed open my door and got out of the car."

(A side note from the editor, Rob Meadows: It is clear that Nicole was lucky that day. A friend, Melissa Houston, died just a few days ago (as of this writing) in an eerily similar accident. She was gone in an instant. We will miss Coach Melissa; she was a tireless advocate for people with leukemia and lymphoma. Nicole was blessed that day, and as you read on, you will see how she is using that blessing to make a real difference in people's lives.)

Dr. Eastman continues…

"This is when a witness approached my car. She said it was the scariest thing she had ever had seen and that I was lucky

to be alive. She said that the truck driver was either trying to get into my lane or get off the freeway at the last minute. The witness saw my vehicle go under the trailer of the truck, even though I could not remember this happening, and if I had not been driving a low-seated car, a 2004 Chrysler Sebring, I could have been decapitated. The front of my vehicle was crumpled and I still don't know how this happened. My witness, a true blessing to me, stayed with me until the state police officer arrived."

In shock, Nicole somehow managed to get into the police car to wait until the EMS arrived. The ambulance sped her to St. John Macomb-Oakland, Macomb Campus in Warren, Michigan – the same hospital where she worked as a resident.

"I remember the back pain starting after I was put on the backboard and when they were wheeling me into the ER, I kept saying, 'I should be dead' over and over. My mother said that the police officer was expecting a fatality and was shocked that I survived such an extreme accident."

"Unfortunately the emergency room physician did not address the concussion symptoms that were present and sent me home almost right away. The accident was at 9:30 in the morning, and I was sent home by 1:30 that day, with no pain medicine. They probably looked me over and thought I was okay. I didn't really have any bruises or even scratches and outside I looked normal but inside I was a mess – more of a mess than I knew."

Tragically, this is a common problem, with the consequences of a blow to the head or other trauma often going underappreciated. A single concussive blow to the head can lead to significant consequences later in life, and a desperate feeling of loss of control.

"After going home from the emergency room, my back and neck pain worsened quickly. I began to experience muscle spasms and severe headaches. I scheduled a follow-up appointment with a family medicine physician for the next day."

"When the next day came I was in so much pain that I could not move and was nauseous. I had no range of motion through my neck or back and I was still experiencing an awful headache. My entire back felt numb. The follow-up appointment with my family physician resulted in over two weeks of muscle relaxant use that made me sleep from 9 PM. until 6 PM. the following day. I had no quality of life. It was almost Christmas, so it was hard to get any rehab or therapy going."

"The pain grew into a severe and constant pain that was taking over my life. And I was in denial. It took a long time to accept what was happening to me, until finally in January I had to, and the doctors did too. While they thought I looked normal at first, when they touched me or tried to inject me they could feel that something was wrong, that I had suffered some serious damage. In a treatment called trigger point injections, they tried to put a needle in my back to relieve the pain and the needle would not even go in - not a good sign."

"I took drugs to relieve the pain and inflammation, and developed stomach ulcers and stomach bleeding due to use of anti-inflammatory medicine. Eventually in April I needed to have spine surgery, and was completely unable to do anything for myself at that point."

"The pain was only one part of the trauma. I also had post-concussive syndrome, including fatigue, memory and

47

concentration issues, and frustration. I still cannot be a passenger in a car – I have to be the driver, still seeking control. I realized that we have a false perception of being in control. During my accident I was not speeding, I was not on my phone and I was not texting. I thought I was in control, that I was doing everything right to protect myself so I would be safe. I was wrong."

"I lost a lot that day. I lost all independence and my sense of self, knowing who I was and being confident that I could do anything. I had been a hyper-independent type A personality, taking care of those around me, and now I could not even take care of myself. Everything that I ever worked for, I had achieved. If not, I would work harder. I was always meticulous, and I always had a plan. Now I could not even stand up, and after spine surgery for three weeks I could not do anything on my own."

"I lost my WSU Physical Medicine and Rehabilitation residency at Oakwood Health Care System due to my inability to start year 2 of my residency on time."

"I watched things being taken away from me, my life being dismantled when after nine years and $225,000 in school loans I could not work."

"I lost the ability to do simple things I once took for granted like household chores, work, and the exercise I had once used for coping."

"Some people who I thought were friends were not. There were people who said to my husband just to divorce me, right from the beginning."

"And I began to realize that I would never be the person I was the day before the accident."

"It was all wiped away."

Like others in the book, Nicole went to a deep, emotional place from which some do not return. What we do there changes the rest of our lives, and affects our families and communities.

"Finally I hit bottom," she said. *"I felt alone and afraid. Nobody knew what I was going through. I watched everything that I worked so hard for fall apart in front of my eyes. I thought it would have been so much easier to have died during that accident."*

"That's when I started to turn things around and get back up again."

"Allowing people to see what I was going through was the start of the journey back up, starting to rebuild. I had to hit the bottom before I could start building a new sense of self. And once I did, people started to reach out to help me, pushing me upward."

"When I opened up and told people on Facebook that it would have been easier to just have died than go through what I do every day, they reached out to help me, letting me know I was not alone. I found support groups on Facebook and I got support to help with my anxiety and post-traumatic stress. My family or friends may have trouble understanding, but others who have been through things like this do understand, and just knowing that helps."

"When I reached the lowest point I also started doing positive self-affirmations and wholeheartedly accepted my faith and

God. I realized that there had to be a purpose for my life and this is when I started rebuilding."

"When I felt completely alone in my bed, unable to take care of myself, I realized that I did not die so I must have work to do still. My purpose here on Earth was not fulfilled, and I needed to do something with the rest of my life."

"In the months since, I'm still recovering. I figured out that I have Ehlers-Danlos Syndrome [hypermobility syndrome], which affects connective tissues and how my body heals. I can't sit or stand for any duration of time without the use of pain management. I have lost the muscle strength in my neck due to the whiplash injury and I also have shoulder instability, musculoskeletal and nerve problems throughout my neck and entire back, inflammation down my spine, and pelvic instability. My rehabilitation has been more difficult due to the fact that I have hypermobility syndrome, which not many people, including physicians, typically address."

Nicole is in a unique position as both a caregiver and a patient, and has a better understanding of the limitations in how doctors treat pain. Nicole knows what patients don't understand, and doctors don't talk about.

Profound events in our lives affect not only us, but our relationships, families, our work, and our communities. Many tragedies are isolating. Treatments make us all look the same. Debilitating pain is often worse. How do our loved ones "see" the pain we have? They can't, not really. They must trust us. They must "go along" with us as we continue to struggle with opening a peanut butter jar, or turning on the water in the kitchen. It is a strain on everyone involved.

"In addition to healing my body, I've been healing my life at home. The day after my accident, my husband said he

wanted a divorce. He said this several times following my accident. So-called friends and even some family members told him to divorce me because they felt he would be happier without me. He did not have any idea of the pain and suffering that I was experiencing both physically and psychologically. He could not understand why his wife – who normally did everything – no longer could even pull clothes from a washing machine or push a vacuum."

"Our counselors have since told us that couples who have been married happily for 30 years and experience this type of trauma have fallen apart. We, however, have put a great deal of effort into making this marriage work, despite all of those who have told us to just give up."

"And I have been healing my mind, working to get back to a place where I know who I am and know that I will be okay. Before, I was the person people turned to at times like when my father died. Now, I'm learning how to turn to others."

"I heard about Louise L. Hay from Hay House Publishing, and bought her Heal Your Life DVD with health affirmations and positive thinking techniques. I watched it twice, crying all the way through, and I felt like there was hope. I knew I could regain a sense of control and chose to make a positive step rather than letting my life fall apart."

"I wrote down affirmations like 'My healing is already in progress'. I believe it now, although I did not in March."

"I wrote down 'Today I will breathe and think positively.' At first I wasn't so sure, but now when I say it, it's true. I have eight affirmations I remind myself of everyday, posted where I can see them when I'm getting ready in the morning."

"When I felt alone, that's when I accepted my faith. Now I know that God is with me, and I know that I'm not alone. I was spiritual before, and grew up Catholic, but now my spiritual side is much stronger. When my dad died in my 3rd year of med school, I watched him accept his fate and die peacefully, which made me believe more in my faith. Now, after facing my own death, I believe even more."

"A friend of mine called me in March to ask how I was doing. He said that I obviously had a reason for living and that maybe I should consider going back to church for a sense of peace. Prior to spinal surgery I submitted a prayer request to Macomb Christian Church; the day before my surgery, both my husband and I attended there together for the first time. Through church we have met some incredibly genuine and service-oriented believers. As for my surgery, I was terrified. I knew too much and I had seen surgical complications and was aware that I too could come out of my surgery more disabled than I already was. A couple of months after my surgery, a woman who knew of me said that she had prayed for me. I felt a sense of gratitude and sincere care: this woman took time from her day to pray for me at a time when she had not even yet met me."

"Finally, I am at the point of acceptance and I truly see myself healing. While I lost a lot that day, I'm also starting to see something new that I might achieve, something I never might have done otherwise."

We all need to know that we can get better. Life is not completely in our control, far from it, but we can choose to find a reason to live, to do something meaningful. And look around – you are not alone. Even when you feel like your world is falling apart, you should know help is out there. Even if life seems impossible right now, there is great growth that can be achieved through adversity, coming out stronger than ever on the other side. It's hard, sometimes incredibly hard. But simply ask yourself if continuing to live in the same way is even harder.

> *"I am now writing to share my experiences and struggles, to offer support and encouragement, and to instill hope and a sense of faith. Writing has given me a new sense of purpose, while I personally continue to heal and recover. I strive to help others realize that they are not alone in their personal struggles. I want to get my story out to people so they don't feel like I felt. Talking, sharing my story, and putting it on my website is my way of letting other people know they are not alone, that there is another person who went through the same thing they are going through."*

> *"People write to me and tell me how inspirational I am, how thankful they are that I write and I share. I almost don't know what to say. It's been a really interesting journey. I understand things I would never have understood before. I know now that I have so much to offer to so many groups of people, things I would never have imagined doing before."*

> *"I am so hoping this is God's plan for me. I am working on my book, arranging it month by month, starting with my wedding vows and walking 12 months in my footsteps. The anticipated title is Breaking Down Barriers. Working through this I'm opening myself to vulnerability, fears, and concerns that I never allowed myself to have before the accident."*

> *"There's so much to do. I want to help other people who have been through accidents like mine. I want to make people more aware of the problem of distracted driving. I*

want to help people prevent strokes like the one that killed my father."

"When I talk to people, so many people share their stories with me now, intimate stories about their lives. Before, I was very confident but I was walled off, and now I've opened up. It does not really matter what the experience is that leads you to the edge, the key is loss of control. We seek control so much that we miss out on many other things life has to offer. Once you realize that there is more to life than your type A realizes, it will either make or break you."

"It's a daily choice".

It's hard working your way back from getting knocked down like this, but easier when you hear from someone like Dr. Eastman, who's been there and made it to the other side. She shows us all that it can be done, that we can all make it through to build a new life for ourselves. It is often said that life is not a destination but a journey. In our mind we plot out our life's journey as a direct line from point A to point B, but it seldom works out that way. There are stops, detours, and moments when the road caves in. Dr. Eastman was in the fast lane, firmly in control, but when she was knocked off course, a new path forward opened up to reveal a greater future.

The journey continues for Dr. Eastman as she explores the new world ahead. As of this writing, Dr. Nicole Eastman is working on her book, she has published works with the World Stroke Campaign and Citi5.org, and she has been speaking to groups in Detroit and New York. She is building her new life, rebuilding her physical health, and reaching out to help others on the road to recovery as well.

You can connect with Nicole and find out more about her book and events at www.drnicolemeastman.com

Chapter 6: Finding the Center

Financial pressure can be intense – so intense that it pushes people to the point where they are ill, where this pressure takes over their lives, sapping away the joy of living. For **Mel Brake**, the pressure led to pain so severe that it immobilized him. But from there Brake began a journey that took his life in a whole new – and far better – direction.

Mel Brake grew up in a working class black family in West Philadelphia and was the first in his family to go to college.

> *"Life was challenging and a struggle at times, and yet I consider myself lucky in many ways,"* Brake said. *"I had my family that I could always rely on, and they've always been very important to me. They have everything to do with who I am, with giving each other the support to make it through everything."*

After college Mel worked for 18 years in sales and marketing. He lived in Springfield, Pennsylvania and worked constantly, only seeing his family and loved ones on weekends, holidays, and a yearly vacation. Like many of us, he spent years in an office sitting at a desk, working for a living.

> *"Working in sales, I had constant monthly sales quotas to meet and never enough staff in the office for support. You had to make your sales quota or you were out the door. You would see people one day at a desk nearby in the office, who would be gone the next. There were constant demands to do*

> *more, to sell more, and there was never enough time in the day to do it."*

> *"I did well in sales over the years, but the pressure never went away, and it just seemed to increase. In fact, the more money I made, the more stressed I became. It wasn't just the quotas – I was pushing myself for more, but the harder I worked, the more I hurt my body. It was like an addiction, with no way to get out, it seemed."*

It's a familiar story: good people who push themselves to the limit working for their family, struggling to make ends meet and maybe even get ahead a little sometime, somewhere. It seems that life is always put off for later, but later never arrives as the years slip by and the years of putting life off until later start to take their toll.

> *"In recent years I worked for a national computer company as an inside sales rep, constantly working the phone and computer. I've always been in pretty good health, generally, but with the relentless pressure from quotas and from myself, and the time spent hunched over my computer, I started to get pain in my neck and down the right side of my body, and through my back."*

> *"In 2007, I was treated by a chiropractor for a work-related stress injury in my neck area, but in 2009 the pain was more severe, in both my neck and back. My chiropractor referred me to a specialist and I would take ibuprofen if I had to, but the pain killers did not help much, and I took them as little as possible because I believe with proper medical treatment the body heals itself."*

> *"By early July 2009 the pain was gradually increasing. I was getting ready for work one day in the morning, but I couldn't do it. I had to stop, go back in the house and lay flat on the*

> *floor, my back frozen. I couldn't even walk, and did my best to avoid moving in any way."*

> *"I felt guilty because I could not make it to work; work was first in my life, and living and family were second."*

This seems to be the typical arc of the lives of many. We start out working for a goal, often for our family, but as time passes the work absorbs us, eating us alive until we forget why we're even there. Some lose the connection with their own life, and it takes a toll on their body as well as their mind. Our body must know that this kind of life cannot go on forever, that something needs to change, even when our mind isn't willing to admit it. For Mel the pain grew in his body until he reached the breaking point, and was propelled suddenly forward to see a new life that lay ahead.

> *"It went on, day after day, and the pain was so constant that I could barely sleep. In August 2009, as I lay in bed one night I experienced a very severe pain in my back and neck, and I thought I was going to die. I prayed that God take me, because the pain was so great I could not live with it any longer. I woke up in the morning after sleeping a little, still in great pain, and I closed my eyes to meditate, to escape from the pain, when something like a door or a tunnel opened."*

The expression "light at the end of tunnel" might be overused, but for many people it is real. Some argue that the image is in our minds because of the ubiquitous media imagery. But these images run deeper than that, back to the beginning of civilization. Such light, such traveling through a connection between this life and another, has been described for centuries in religious texts of many faiths. It is not just a Hollywood concept – it is a human one.

> *"I could see light rushing past me as I left my body and traveled through the tunnel. I was moving down the tunnel*

with moving, very dynamic, green, blue, and violet lights. Like a Kaleidoscope: big bold colors, rotating. I let myself go, and did not know what was happening, but felt these beautiful lights rushing past me. I was moving toward a center, which was black with some white light, and then green and purple. It seemed like it went on forever."

Like our previous story from Rob Meadows, Mel finds himself at an interstitial space, a place between here and there. Perhaps it is a place of judgment, a place of respite and reflection, or a place of redemption.

"When I reached the end of the tunnel, I knew it was also the beginning of a new life. I found myself in a large black space. It was not heaven or hell, but somewhere else. I cannot explain where or what it was except that I was not afraid. I was not happy either really, just calm and watching, listening. All was quiet, absolutely still, with nothing moving. I felt like I was at the center of something, at the center of everything, and everything was without limits. I could feel the space all around me in this place and although I was this new self, I was not afraid."

"In this place there was an enormous block that was black, and everything else was black as well – no colors. I felt that the box was the center of the center. Then, there was a figure, a large head and face that I knew was me, and there was a syringe in my neck."

"I said in my mind, 'Where am I? Who are you?' The being said, 'I am knowing'. There was no one I could see, just a presence I felt in all this void and darkness that told me I was not alone, that this awareness was there with me."

"I was more than consciousness during this experience, I was super-consciousness. I knew when I woke up that I would be all right. Seeing myself being healed, and knowing the higher presence, I knew when I woke up I would be healed. When I woke up the pain was there, but it was reduced enough that I could sit up and move around. I was not given a message or a direction, but I knew clearly and certainly I would get better."

"Within a couple of weeks the pain that I had for many months was gone, and my wanting to die left me after that night. I believe that my time here on this planet was not at its end, and that "I am knowing" sent me back for Her own reasons."

"I felt like I died that day. I felt like a different person when I woke up, a new person. I felt like Ebenezer Scrooge, like I had a new lease on life. I had awakened."

"In the months that followed I continued with my chiropractor, although I did not tell him about the experience. When the experience first happened, I was reluctant to talk about it with anybody, even my family. I did not have a reference point, did not know what had happened, and did not know how to talk about it. Now that it's been two years, it's still not easy, but I'm more comfortable."

"All I know is that something happened to me that I did not understand and still don't understand; an event that changed how I live my life, and how I do many things."

Mel's experience was unique, and yet he shares much in common with others I've talked with in this book. He was in need of a change in his life, and the universe delivered it. Finding a clear space, he was given awareness of a new life ahead, and knew he had to make the most of this new life. And like the others, this meant he needed to do work that had meaning, reaching out beyond his own needs to help others. For Mel, this meant getting involved with kids in his community who needed help and had few other options to turn to; kids who badly needed to see that they are valuable people themselves, with something unique to say and something unique to give to the world.

> *"After that day I went back to work in September or so, and not long after they laid me off as a result of the down economy. I was not even disappointed – I was grateful. I had already wanted to do something different with myself, and this was my chance. I needed to do more with my life than chasing dollars, so I moved on from the '9 to 5' mind set. I wanted to work with kids, and this was my chance to make a greater contribution, other than just making money."*

> *"I started my non-profit the following spring, the MPW Foundation (Mel's Poetry Works) in which I teach children from troubled homes about improving self-esteem as well as life-building skills through artistic workshops."*

Mel's workshops offer poetry, music, painting, and singing classes with lesson plans focused on self-esteem building. They help students to express themselves through art.

> *"I am finally doing what I love. I am finally living my life as who I am."*

> *"I had always liked performing. When I was 5 I had put on shows for other kids in the neighborhood. Over the last five years I had started reading poetry that I had written publicly. After I was laid off I could start working with art and poetry with kids. I talked with my brother, who wanted to start a*

foundation to work with children. The idea came to me, that this was something that I could do."

"When I created the MPW Foundation (Mel's Poetry Works), I started contacting schools and the YMCA, and giving out programs. I went from working for others for money to working for myself by helping others. To build up the non-profit, I started volunteering my services to other organizations in my area such as summer camps and afterschool programs."

Troubled kids tend to fall through the cracks when they don't have money or strong family support, and often they don't get a second chance. Mel was lucky in many ways growing up because of his close family, but he says that he can easily relate to these kids from growing up in a working class background.

"I went to college, the first in my family, and I was self-driven, but there were still many challenges. I see things in their eyes, the trouble that they face, and I know they don't have the kind of support system they need to deal with these things."

"My nephew, for example, was getting in trouble with the family, so I told him that he should try to write about what happened, about what he was feeling. He would write, I would read and critique it, and I helped him publish it online. It must have been the first time he really did something creative like this, expressing himself with his words. Before, he did not think that he was anyone, did not think he mattered, until he found through his writing that he had something to say and people would listen."

"This is what I do. I give the kids a voice, and they learn how to listen and be non-judgmental. I'm like Fred Rogers on the

> *road. I love how he spoke to kids, how he let them know they are special. To work with these kids, I go where they are: to the libraries, youth centers, and schools. Kids need this more than ever and yet there is less support available than ever as budgets are cut. There is a huge gap in the funding available compared to what is needed."*

In the future Mel would like to present as many as 100 workshops a year throughout the Philadelphia area. For today, he is very happy with his life, inside and outside.

> *"Something was lacking in my life before. When I think about it back then, two years ago, my life had no purpose. I came home every day from work, had dinner, and saw my family rarely. I'm afraid I would not have changed without these events, this experience; I would just have continued on the same path. Now I have a purpose, a direction, and it's greater than myself. I'm doing something concrete for others. Now, today, I have a greater appreciation for every day. I wake up grateful, appreciating life, living, family, and friends."*

> *"The best part of my life now, the crescendo that my work leads up to, is when I am standing in front of kids in programs that are fun, where they're learning, and they're receiving. Everything in my life leads up to this. At that moment, with the kids, it's like I'm back at the center of everything from that moment in my experience. That moment contains everything I am completely."*

Like many others in this book, Mel's experience has given him serenity with respect to dying, the potential of an afterlife and mortality.

> *"One thing that has changed since the experience is that before I was afraid of death, but now I'm not. I don't welcome*

death, but I don't think about it any longer. The experience was like opening a door, and walking through, like changing clothes. And I see now death is like this: it is not the end of anything, but the beginning – one step in a journey, like crossing a river from one place to another. I know there is more to death than meets the eye."

"Since then I have a sense that there is much more to life than what we can taste, see, know, or feel. I know that there is something greater than me, you, or us. I know that after death, life does not end. I know that death is like changing one's clothes. That life is really a profound mystery."

Mel's story is amazing and unique, but he isn't alone in the crushing pain and stress he felt from his work and his life. The amazing part came when he found a way to let go of his old life and build a better one, released from the stress and embraced by a higher purpose that buoys him up rather than piling an ever-greater burden on his shoulders. It's even more amazing how much of a difference reaching out to help others can make in our lives.

With the MPW Foundation, Mel Brake works with troubled kids, giving them a chance to express themselves and build a new life of their own. He is working to develop a new program called "Dare to Dream," and donations at GoFundMe.com to support the foundation and its work are always welcome. Kids like those that Mel works with often have nowhere else to go. Finding a cause like this that we can commit to, people we can make a real difference for, gives our lives the deeper meaning and purpose we all need. By finding this purpose we can finally heal our minds and our bodies, becoming whole again in a way that nothing else seems able to achieve.

To read more about Mel's story and upcoming events, check his blog at:

http://melbrake.wordpress.com/

Chapter 7: Founding IHadCancer.com

Coming to the US as a child, **Mailet Lopez** has worked hard to overcome many obstacles. She was the first in her family to go to college, and she rose rapidly in the burgeoning world of internet media. None of this prepared her for the struggle with breast cancer that hit her in 2008, but when she found the help she needed in other patients, she also found how she could make a difference for millions of other people facing cancer.

When Mailet Lopez came to the US from a small town in Cuba, it was a huge leap for her and her whole family. She was a young child and spoke little English, and her family was leaving behind everything they knew except for each other; like countless others, they came to the US in pursuit of a dream, with the hope of doing more for their family.

> *"When I was still only a child my family fled the Fidel Castro regime as part of the Mariel boatlift in 1980,"* said Lopez. *"My parents fled with only three days notice, coming to the US to chase the American Dream. Although it was a difficult decision, my parents wanted my sister and me to have opportunities that would not have been available if we had stayed in Cuba."*

When her family came to the US they arrived in New York, where Mailet grew up on Long Island. Although the US attracts millions with the hope of a brighter future, reaching your dreams is seldom quick or easy. Mailet and her family were in it for the long run – determined to work hard, stick together, and stick with it.

> *"Sometimes it was difficult for a family of exiles who did not speak English and had little money,"* she said, *"but my parents worked hard and we all helped each other."*

Her parents did whatever work they could find, her dad doing construction work one day and factory work another. They lived in a huge house with her cousins and other relatives; even with all of their work and sacrifice it was hard sometimes and money was tight, but they always managed.

> *"My parents shielded me, I think; later I found out what a hard time they had, having to choose between paying the rent one month, or the electricity, or the water, but I was not aware of all of this then."*

Regardless of their money at the time, she had big dreams for her life and her family always supported her. Some parents might think their kids have crazy, unrealistic dreams, and maybe they do, but her parents never minimized her hopes and dreams. Maybe they knew somehow that minimizing a person's dreams can't help but bring down the person as well. They believed in her without a doubt and were not afraid to let her know it, encouraging her to aim high in life, no matter what.

> *"My father would support anything I wanted to do, any interests I had. In high school I talked about having a company, or having a restaurant, and nobody ever told me I was crazy. From the beginning, with my parents' support I thought I would start a business."*

Mailet went to college at Hofstra University. She was the first in her family to graduate from college in 1998, studying graphics design with art and computer classes. This was a time when art, design, and computers were all coming together with the rise of the internet, providing the unique opportunity for people at the right time and place – with the right talent – to join in the meteoric rise of the web, helping businesses present their best face to the world through the internet.

In this exciting young industry, Mailet soared.

> *"After college I immediately entered the digital world and began my career at one of the first web development agencies in New York City,"* said Mailet.

She was doing well enough that while having lunch in New York with the VP of sales at the agency, Anthony Del Monte, they found themselves talking about starting their own business. It wasn't a question of 'if' – it was only a question of 'when.'

> *"It wasn't just idle conversation,"* said Mailet. *"Anthony was great with clients and had a passion for what he did, and I saw that drive and interest and I thought that he would be excellent in his own company."*

As it happened, their lunch was at the World Trade Center in New York and the date was September 10th, 2001. The events of the next day made the decision for her. Within a few weeks their old company was out of business in the chaos that followed 9/11, and their new business, Squeaky Wheel Media, was born.

As a partner and project manager in the new business, Mailet focused on building websites that work well for people, giving them what they need in the easiest, most direct, and most appealing way.

> *"We grew Squeaky from a fledgling startup to an award-winning agency that builds online presences for leading corporations and brands. The company grew until we had 30*

> *designers and technologists and were awarded Small Agency of the Year for Best Culture from AdAge."*

Everything was going incredibly well, better than Mailet had even hoped. Then, like for so many in this book, her life was derailed. In 2008, she was diagnosed with breast cancer.

> *"When I was first diagnosed, the doctors wanted to rush me right in to surgery,"* said Mailet. *"One doctor wanted to do a mastectomy while another one wanted to do a lumpectomy, and either way they wanted to do it right away, in a matter of days. It was all too fast for me to absorb. Anyone who's been diagnosed with cancer will tell you it's a roller coaster."*

Leaping into action might help to still fears, and sometimes cancer requires quick action, but acting out of fear and getting swept off your feet doesn't always lead to the best decision. Taking time to get off the fast track and think can reveal a new path that was hidden, maybe even a better path.

> *"I was overwhelmed by the cancer diagnosis and I needed time. To slow things down I bought myself three weeks, saying I had a new office I had to move into. I used the time to read, to talk with people, and connect with new ideas and therapies to take more control over what was happening with my body."*

Having so many people telling you what they think you should do – and having so many decisions to make – cannot be a great feeling. Knowing the cancer is silently growing, the clock ticking, can make it feel for cancer patients like they're losing control of their lives, stuck between the cancer, their doctors, and everyone else. And feeling like you're losing control, like a leaf in the wind, makes everything (including your health) worse.

> *"Lacking control is one of the biggest problems for a lot of patients I think,"* said Mailet. *"They often feel stuck on a runaway train with the medical system, at the mercy of a chosen course of action. Giving people back a sense of control is important."*

More and more patients are getting actively involved in decisions about their medical care, actively looking for new options and questioning their doctors and others about the best way to go. In Mailet's case, she decided to get a lumpectomy rather than mastectomy. After her surgery, her doctors wanted her to start chemotherapy and radiation; however, after reading and talking to people she started trying a wide variety of therapies, some of them a bit off of the beaten track of standard cancer treatment. A side benefit of doing this is that she reclaimed control over her life and her body, improving her state of mind as well.

> *"I did something called Escozul treatment from blue scorpion venom, acupuncture, supplements, and a vegan or vegetarian diet. I could not control everything that was going on, but I was doing anything I could do, controlling the stuff I could control."* It was her life and nobody else's.

One of the biggest criticisms of modern medicine is that it often treats the symptoms of the body, but fails to deal with the whole person. This was expressed very clearly in a previous story from Dr. Nicole Eastman, who has seen the health care system from both a patient's and caregiver's perspective.

All too often our health care processes ignore the crucial role that the people around us play in influencing our health. We are social creatures and need social connections, even more so when we are facing a great challenge. And some of the most valuable connections for cancer patients might be with the only people who can really relate to what they are going through: other cancer patients.

> *"Although I had wonderful doctors and plenty of support from family and friends, I was missing the connection to someone who shared my experiences firsthand,"* said Mailet. *"Only someone who had gone through cancer could offer the particular type of support I was looking for during that difficult time."*

People who have dealt with cancer have the practical knowledge that only comes from very hard won experience. They didn't read about cancer in a magazine or a book. They lived it 24/7. Other patients can talk about doctors, therapies, and other resources, and provide a strongly sympathetic ear so patients feel a little less afraid and alone. Another's perspective can also reveal alternative treatment options.

> *"One of the biggest steps I took with my therapy happened when I talked with a woman who told me about an alternative to high-dose chemotherapy,"* said Mailet. *"She told me about a low-dose type of chemo treatment called IPT, insulin potentiation therapy. Cancer cells are hungry; they love sugar and have more receptors than normal cells. IPT takes advantage of this by lowering your insulin level before administering the chemo. Your insulin level is then brought back up, giving the cancer cells a field day as they go after the chemo [while] leaving the normal healthy cells out of it. This way you can use much lower doses of chemotherapy drugs, so there are fewer side effects."*

While normal chemotherapy kills normal cells in many parts of the body as well as cancer cells, IPT therapy is often able to selectively kill cancer cells with lower levels of chemotherapy agents, leaving the rest of the body healthier than with standard chemotherapy. As a new therapy, insulin potentiation therapy is not widely accepted in the medical community yet. It can take years, decades even, for new therapies like this to be widely accepted and used; data is gathered, studies are published, and minds are changed, but patients don't have decades to wait. If Mailet had not actively gone out looking for new treatment options, talking to other patients to see what they had come across, odds are she probably wouldn't have discovered IPT. Making this connection changed the direction of her cancer treatment.

It takes a brave person to take back control of their treatment when dealing with cancer, sometimes going against the recommendations of their doctors, but there's a lot at stake, both mentally and physically. Ultimately, the decision is the patient's.

> *"Once I decided to move forward with IPT, I told my oncologist I would not be doing regular chemotherapy and she wasn't too happy, but it was what I wanted. I stayed much healthier through the chemotherapy treatments, with few side effects, and the cancer today is gone. A year after my surgery when saw my surgeon, the doctor scolded me for not following the conventional treatment plan. When I came back again later, he asked, 'Are you still doing that stuff?' He said, 'I guess this stuff is working for you.' He had to admit it when he saw that I was doing well. I was back in control again rather than having the cancer running my life."*

Soon, other people started getting referred to her to talk about this treatment and about their experience with cancer. As Mailet's health improved, she started to see how she could help other people facing cancer. Just as the woman she had talked with had helped her to regain control of her treatment and her life by giving her more information and options, so she wanted to help other people as well. Mailet thought of simply doing a blog about her experiences, but this didn't seem like enough. She needed a way to reach more people, and to have it be larger than her own experiences. From this, IHadCancer.com was born.

> *"I recognized the need for a connection to someone battling my same condition and imagined a way to create these connections," Mailet said. "Anthony encouraged me to write and speak about it, and the idea grew from there. Rather than just a blog, the IHadCancer.com site let me expand this for all types of cancer, and not just for breast cancer. Breast cancer is important, but there are many other problems, particularly rare cancers, where it is crucial that people have someone to talk to. I created IHadCancer.com so that survivors, fighters, and supporters can connect, share information and become more empowered patients."*

> *"IHadCancer.com is a social network for cancer patients, giving them an easy way to connect with each other and help each other beat cancer. People share information, encouragement, and just plain understanding when they're having a hard time."*

Having someone to talk openly with, someone who's been there before, and seeing that others have fought cancer and won, helps cancer patients to see that they can get through it, and helps them keep up their hope. Just going to the site and reading what others have to say can help, even if a patient isn't ready to jump in and get involved on the site. By approaching their doctors with more information, patients gain more control over their future, something that has been shown to improve health all on its own.

> *"They won't all use the same therapy and everyone should talk to their doctor, but I know that many people will be helped by being better informed and by having other people they can talk with who share their experiences," said Mailet. "By*

> *having more information, patients are fighters rather than victims, fighting for themselves and taking informed question to their doctors. You are so alone in this process that just talking to someone, knowing there is help, puts you back in control."*

People often don't like talking about cancer, out of fear it seems, and one of the benefits of connecting with others at IHadCancer.com is breaking down this taboo barrier and dispelling some of the fear.

> *"Over time, the more comfortable people are, the better it is for the person dealing with it. Sometimes people feel angry, powerless, or alone, and they can express this in our 'Dear Cancer' section on the site, getting these feelings out there rather than keeping it bottled in,"* said Mailet. *"It's hard to write some of these things down, to get them out there, but afterward it helps."*

It's been a long trip, but the I Had Cancer site is growing quickly, reaching more people, and Mailet is doing well, cancer-free and excited about her future.

> *"I didn't know my strength until I had cancer, and was forced to do more than I ever thought I could. You become a stronger person."*

Not many of us would choose to go through cancer treatment, but having been there and survived has allowed Mailet to take this important new direction in her life for herself and countless others.

> *"1.5 million people are diagnosed with cancer each year, and every one of them is going to face a challenge. That is a lot of people who need help. I think we have something powerful, something that is desperately needed. It's all about reaching people and helping them to reach each other."*

Millions of people face cancer and yet many of them feel like they are alone. It makes so much sense to reach out to others to face challenges like this together. The benefits are many and with tools like IHadCancer.com, connecting with others is far easier for those who are willing to give it a try. If you're recovering from cancer, dealing with it now, or know someone who is, go to IHadCancer.com to find support and connect with others who've been there and know what it's all about.

To find out more and get involved, visit www.IHadCancer.com.

Chapter 8: SoapBox Therapy Pioneer

I think most of us would agree that brain surgery is a pretty big deal, and **Brooke Miller** has been through major brain surgery not once but twice. The second time around, she decided that the universe was trying very hard to tell her something and it was time to listen up. She realized that she had a greater purpose she was working toward and that she still had far more to do if she was really going to make a difference in the mental health problems affecting so many people.

One of the big steps in Brooke's journey came just before her 14th birthday.

> *"I was 13 years old and hanging out with friends at the house of a boy that I had a big crush on when I began to have a horrible headache above my left eye,"* recalled Brooke. *"I took aspirin and waited a while, but the symptoms wouldn't go away. I ended up calling my mom and telling her I needed to come home, that I was in horrible pain and didn't know what to do. The reason she knew this was serious: because I don't take having a crush on someone very lightly."*

Very quickly it was clear that this was a serious problem, not your average headache or migraine.

> *"I ended up seeing a ton of different doctors, and even being told by one of them that I had brain cancer, with no testing to prove this. My mom was a mess and I was scared out of my mind. We ended up at Children's Hospital Chicago with no*

> *appointment, and somehow, my mom was able to get us in with an amazing doctor who calmed our minds and did further testing. My tumor ended up being something called Langerhans cell histiocytosis (LCH) in my skull."*

Langerhans cell histiocytosis involves an unusual proliferation of immune cells, and is often seen in children. In Brooke's case, the tumor was growing so rapidly that it was quickly growing towards her brain and needed to be removed immediately before things got worse.

> *"I had surgery the week after they identified what the tumor was, as it was puncturing my skull and growing rapidly towards my brain. It needed to be removed ASAP. I didn't need follow-up treatment like chemo or radiation, thank goodness. The recovery was about five days in the hospital and a summer at home. A lot of the recovery was emotional, given I was about to be a freshman girl and had half a head of hair. It made me stronger and more confident for sure."*

The surgery was not easy, but it went well: the abnormal growth was removed and no further problems related to the surgery were seen for many years, all the way through high school and college. While the surgery faded in her memory, she realized she needed to deal with mental health issues that had become a factor over the years, not from the surgeries but from other aspects of her inner life. As Brooke did this, going through therapy and seeing how helpful it was for her, she realized that she wanted to be more than a mental health patient. She wanted to become a therapist so she could reach out to help others just as she had been helped. Studying the inner workings of the mind felt right to her, like it was the direction she was meant to take in her life.

> *"In my 20s I dealt with intense self-esteem issues as well as a very unhealthy relationship with food and my body. I entered therapy with hopes of feeling better and moving forward with my life. I connected so deeply with the process that I applied to graduate school, not knowing much about psychology in general, but having a gut feeling I was in the right place."*

Ultimately Brooke studied psychotherapy at the Pacifica Graduate Institute, becoming a licensed marriage and family therapist (MFT). After getting married in September of 2007, Brooke also started to develop her career as a psychotherapist.

Then, while on a trip to Mexico with her husband in March of 2008, she woke up one day with a pain above one of her eyes, giving her a really bad feeling as she remembered her health issues from many years previous. When she looked in the mirror, the feeling got even worse.

> *"I felt it while still lying in bed and could feel a little pea-shaped hard ball over my eyebrow. My stomach dropped and I just knew. I looked in the mirror and the ball was visible just by looking at me. I was terrified. My husband was in denial and said I must have bumped my head in the middle of the night. I vomited on the plane on our way home, and knew in every cell of my being that this was happening yet again. The body just remembers."*

They had only been married a short time, and Brooke found herself thrown into doubt, fear, and confusion as she had to shed light on her first brain surgery for her husband.

> *"We got to the sickness and health stuff pretty quickly,"* said Brooke.

When they returned to the US it was clear that brain surgery would once again be needed, whatever the source of the mass was. Brooke went on to experience her second brain surgery; the mass was removed, and was identified not as cancer or LCH, but a rare infection that had probably gotten started all those years earlier in 1994, during the first brain surgery. There had been no so sign of anything wrong until the infection broke out above Brooke's eyebrow along with severe pain.

The second surgery went well, but its impact extended far beyond the surgery itself. The shock of resurgent brain issues led Brooke to rethink many things.

> *"The first surgery, which was in 1994, sent me the message that life is fragile and you'd better live it well, but this surgery sent me a stronger message: You think you're living well, but you must be kidding me if you think you're living up to your full potential. There is so much more to you and it's a disservice that you're keeping it all to yourself!"*

Mental health is an important problem for millions, but people can be afraid to talk about it even with friends and family for fear of how they will be perceived. Additionally, mental health professionals are not always skilled at speaking publicly about the field in a simple, engaging, and approachable way. After her second surgery, Brooke saw that she had a greater purpose: to become more outspoken beyond her private therapy practice, founding SoapBox Therapy to reach a much larger audience and take on mental health challenges in a bigger way.

> *"I knew I had a larger message and a bigger voice, and I needed to add a component to my career that included being out of the therapy room and reaching the masses. I had been holding myself back because I thought I was in a vocation in*

which it wasn't appropriate to make a lot of noise – this proved untrue. I was no longer willing to hold myself back for anyone."

"Since starting my blog and my media career efforts, I've been welcomed, complimented, and embraced. Being a psychotherapist both on the couch and off has proven to be the exact balance I so desperately wanted."

Going through this big challenge changed how Brooke sees the world and how she sees her clients, with greater appreciation for the fears they face.

"I love talking about my surgery, as it reminds me that there is a reason I'm still standing. Every day my job is to make sure that I do my life justice. I can also connect with my clients in a deeper way than I ever was able to before. I've been there, I've been scared, I went to bed one night and thought I might die and had to think about if that was okay with me or not. I thought about my life and what I would do differently and how I would be better – to others, but mostly to myself. I can sit with people who come to therapy and understand what they mean when they say they have no hope and that it's debilitating. And I also know what it feels like to come out the other side."

Often after coming through big challenges like Brooke, the people in this book view their life differently, including the big problems life threw at them. Brooke came to see her surgeries as opportunities because they forced her to rethink her life and strive for a greater purpose.

"Whether it's brain surgery or a fight with a relative, there's a way to say 'thank you to the experience rather than saying, 'I wish that never happened.'"

It would have been easy to see herself as a victim, to see the challenges as an unfair problem thrown her way and feel angry about it, but she did not want to go down that path. It seemed like a waste of time and a distraction from the greater work to be done.

> *"If I wasn't grateful about my surgery then I would spend a lot of time and energy being angry, wishing things were different, being mad at the world, at my body, at my doctors. The tumor would, essentially, win. By being grateful that I was given this opportunity to be a more whole, well-rounded person, I'm not wasting any energy. I'm relaxed. And I'm a better person. It's a choice. Either be pissed and lose time, or be grateful and gain. It's easier said than done, simply because we're trained to complain and be upset about things. But if you choose not to follow the social rules, you might just get a lot out of your challenges."*

Looking forward, Brooke sees big challenges ahead for all of the millions who deal with mental health, whether in themselves or someone they know – but there are also big opportunities to make a difference.

> *"The big mental health problems facing us are expansive, but what I find is that most of them come from a history of not being seen for who you really are, or heard for what you're really saying. Many if not all of my clients were told in some form or another, that they needed to be different than they were in order to get the attention and love that they wanted or deserved. Then, they lived their lives acting the way they thought they were supposed to, rather than the way they truly were. Years of deep inauthenticity and self-doubt can really do a number on someone. It affects their ability to trust, to communicate, to be vulnerable, and to be emotionally healthy."*

By continuing to develop her outreach, Brooke might just help to create exactly the kind of difference that is needed.

> *"I want to see therapy modernized and I want to see people change for the better and live in a happier, healthier, more balanced world. I would love to change the world, making it a more emotionally intelligent place. Check back soon. I'll let you know how it's going."*

Mental health challenges are often hidden, unseen, and untreated because people are afraid of how they will be judged. When Brooke had this challenge in her life, she used it as an inspiration, a message from the universe that it was time to rise to the greater challenge. Having help from someone like Brooke can make all the difference to those who are facing these challenges alone. In turn, some of those who seek help may find ways to help others as well, connecting with the greater good to speed their own progress.

As of this writing, Brooke Miller is posting regular video blogs, working on her book, taking care of her newborn baby, and talking with patients to make the world a more emotionally healthy place.

Check in with her progress at www.soapboxtherapy.com

Contact Brooke at: brooke@soapboxtherapy.com

Chapter 9: Creator of Whatchyagot Bags

It's been said that every problem that comes our way is a chance to learn, and I've said this myself on more than one occasion, but some of life's lessons are hard to handle. For **Julie Gallegos**, a barrage of hard times left her full of fear and anxiety, with no idea what to do. She struggled to find an answer, but it wasn't until she surrendered and accepted all that had happened that she saw where she was going. Inspired by her father's battle with cancer, she saw how she could help him and countless others, and rebuild her own life along the way.

Julie has been through a lot in recent years, more than anyone should be asked to deal with. Her son was diagnosed with cancer in 2006 (now in remission). Her sister died in 2007, her mom in 2008, and her niece just months later. The year after, her stepbrother and cousin died, and for years her father struggled with advanced cancer and heart disease – his doctors were amazed at his resilience. In addition to the challenges in her family, Julie's career stalled, going over the edge along with the whole mortgage industry in 2008. To top it all off, her marriage of 25 years dissolved in the stress of everything that was happening. It's enough to make anyone rethink their life, questioning where they are going and what they are doing with the time they're given here.

It was a hard time and Julie struggled, wondering why this was all happening to her, one bad thing after another. At times it seemed like too much to bear. It didn't seem fair.

> *"As all of these things in my life happened, I seriously did not know how I was going to move forward or what I would do,"* said Julie. *"I didn't want to live and I didn't want to die. I felt like I was trapped in the middle, unable to move either forward or backward."*

Through all of this, as Julie struggled to come to terms with her circumstances, her father continued his long struggle with cancer – it was a difficult journey but also a huge inspiration.

> *"I could write an entire book on his life alone,"* said Julie. *"He endured stage four cancer for eight years. While in the hospital after his initial rectal surgery, he had a heart attack and had to have open heart surgery, then shortly after surgery [he] contracted a staph infection in his chest so bad that they had to remove his sternum and move his pectoral muscles to cover the area of the sternum and protect the heart. After this he had chemo each year for eight months out of the year and sometimes radiation too. His cancer continued to spread to his colon, liver, lungs and then stomach and spine. His doctors said they had never seen a patient live as long with so much treatment and continue to press forward with such a strong will to live."*

One of the problems her father faced during the years of his extensive treatment was that it was difficult for him to go out anywhere, even to family events. Because of his surgery and cancer, he had a colostomy and medicines that would need to be taken care of when he went out. Her father would leave events after only 30 minutes because he was unsure about managing his colostomy bag, as well as associated equipment and supplies.

Thinking of her father, the new path for her to move forward came to her. Julie saw what she would do with her life. She might not be able to cure his condition, but she could help him live better, making him more at ease when out of the house or the hospital. Further, if she could do it for him, she could help the countless other people in the world like cancer patients, who have trouble going out with their medicines and supplies. When she searched for a bag that her father could use to carry his supplies, she couldn't find one, so she decided to make one, committing herself to that goal.

> *"I decided after researching for bags and not finding one, to design the bag I envisioned so he could carry what he needed with confidence and privacy for all of his personal items."*

Julie designed the so-called WhatchyaGot Bag to hold important things like medicines and keep them organized, rather than tossing them in a jumble inside a regular bag. She designed the bag for people like her dad, with an insulated pocket for medications that need to be kept cool while away from home, such as insulin for people with diabetes. The design with straps on the inside keeps other medications organized and easy to find. Although Julie designed the bags for people with medical concerns, the bags are also catching on with others like busy parents or travelers, because they work so well to carry bottles, milk, snacks, liquids, gels, and even damp or wet items. As people tried the bag, they let Julie know how grateful they were that her creation helped them lead a better life when so much else about their life was hard.

> *"A little thing like this can make a difference for people, giving them renewed freedom. The elderly people that call me tell me how the bag has made them more comfortable and free to leave their homes, that the bag gives them a sense of freedom and confidence to travel anywhere, whether to their doctor's appointment, to the grocery store or on a vacation.*

> *It's such a rewarding feeling, knowing I am doing something that is helping others."*

Along the way, Julie found that she was doing more than creating a bag. She was creating the new life she had been looking for, the life she needed so deeply to move her life forward again. The more she has given through her efforts to develop her new business, the more that has been returned.

> *"I have spent countless nights awake wanting to put something together to help others in a bigger way,"* said Julie. *"I've always been generous with time and money, whether it was taking the elderly to appointments, giving money to strangers, providing Christmas for a family, paying for a stranger's lunch, or donating items to homeless shelters. I believe I'm here to make an impact in some way."*

It took time for Julie to work through everything that was going on in her life, but she feels now that she's on a better path in many ways, and it feels right, as if this is what she had been looking for all along.

> *"I've experienced a lot of grief and illness, but now that I have this work with the WhatchyaGot Bag, I feel better about my life,"* said Julie. *"I'm feeling well, finally, after learning a lot along the way about life and love. It changed the way I look at life. I learned gratitude instead of pity. I learned how much life has to offer and that I can get through difficult situations that I never thought I had the ability to handle – especially by myself. I had to learn to change my attitude and thoughts and not stay stuck in the past. I've learned to persevere, to never give up."*

Having been down that road, people like Julie see the immense reward of reaching out to the many others around us who share our world, each with their own story and difficulties.

"I want to help others who have experienced tragedies because I understand – I've been there and I offer the kind of support that's hard if you haven't been there. I believe my story can inspire countless people on their quest towards healing and becoming their best self, in spite of any extraordinary circumstances. While the road to inner peace and acceptance may seem daunting and formidable, I am living proof that with desire, faith, and determination we can turn tragedy into triumph."

Julie's had a long journey, and it's far from over. While I was working on this book, Julie told me that her father, the inspiration for her new life, had died early in 2012 after battling cancer for a very long time. He sounds like a brave and great man. Likewise, Julie is a brave woman who has overcome a great deal to move toward a powerful new life and new business built firmly on the foundation of finding ways to help others who are dealing with problems like those her father faced.

Julie continues working hard to help others through her business and the rest of her life, inspired by her father and many others who have faced adversity with bravery, resilience, and grace. To find out more about Julie and WhatchyaGot Bags, you can visit her website and get in touch with her at www.whatchyagotbags.com.

Chapter 10: Building a Healthier World

Dave Alberga loves fitness, and not just because he's built his life around it. As the CEO of Active Network in San Diego, Dave is a strong proponent of fitness in his company, his community, the nation, and the world. Even before joining Active Network in 1999, Dave had always been a lover of outdoor activities, including cycling, skiing, and scuba. What he hadn't counted on was how the onset of ulcerative colitis would lead him in new directions to encourage wellness for others and find a cure for colitis.

When I met with Dave in his office in San Diego, looking out over buildings, freeways, trees, and hills, he reflected on his experience with inflammatory bowel disease (IBD) and coming back after the surgery. As the CEO of Active in San Diego, Dave has had some big challenges come his way. Active provides registration and other technology systems for many outdoor activities and parks, and has grown significantly in recent years, despite a few bumps along the way. One of the biggest challenges he's faced, though, was dealing with severe ulcerative colitis. He's very fit, and although he's the CEO, he wore a t-shirt, looking like he was ready for a run. It was hard to believe that not so long ago he had been brought so near the edge of death due to colitis.

> *"I was moderately symptomatic for 17 years,"* Alberga said, floor-to-ceiling windows behind him.

His colitis was not severe at first, allowing him to adjust and handle it without addressing it with others. Then, little by little, his condition got worse until his life revolved around it.

> *"They boiled the frog on me, with the IBD slowly getting worse, one degree at a time. Slowly your life gets so compromised over time that you hardly notice. And my life was pretty compromised. The reality is that people with colitis know where every restroom is within 100 yards at all times."*

Ulcerative colitis involves chronic inflammation of the colon in the large intestine, causing abdominal pain, diarrhea, and blood loss, depending on its severity. It's not something people like to talk about – and for the most part they don't. As a result, the surprisingly common and serious condition often flies under the radar, relatively unnoticed.

> *"It's a humiliating disease and one that you can hide, so you do,"* Alberga said, matter-of-factly. *"There is a core set of diseases where it's okay to talk about it and you get support, but because of the nature of IBD, you can hide it and you do hide it, and there's really no support."*

Over the years Alberga dealt with ulcerative colitis, he managed the symptoms and his life to minimize its impact. But little by little the symptoms got worse, until he had a life threatening flare-up in 2000. The 6' 1" CEO dropped from an athletic 182 pounds to 137 pounds. Hospitalized because of excessive bleeding, he had nine blood transfusions and his doctors recommended the total removal of his colon.

> *"By 2000 it just blew up and inflamed my entire gut,"* Dave said. *"I went into the hospital, and was put on steroids. I was just hemorrhaging; it was really bad. Then when it looked like*

> *maybe it was under control, I left. Two days later I was right*
> *back in the hospital."*

Because his colitis had been slowly getting worse over time, and he'd managed to deal with it for so many years, he still believed that he could keep on managing it in a similar way.

> *"In my mind at this point I was thinking, 'I've gotten over flare-*
> *ups before,' until the doctors said, 'There's nothing else we*
> *can do for you. You can decide to have surgery or not, but if*
> *you wait too long it might be too late.'"*

Alberga found himself facing a big choice. With surgery, his entire colon would be removed; with the source of the inflammation permanently removed, his health would improve. But he hesitated, afraid what this surgery would mean for his life. With his colon removed, he feared he would no longer be able to lead the great life that he wanted.

We don't hear much about colitis in the news or see many public figures talking about it, but Dave's wife Christine had heard the story of local sports legend Rolf Benirschke, a professional football player who was a placekicker for the San Diego Chargers from 1978 to 1987. After collapsing on a team flight in 1979, he was hospitalized with severe colitis, and his large intestine removed. After surgery, Benirschke used ostomy bags to collect waste, and continued to play football for years. Rolf has also been an outspoken proponent for fighting colitis, creating the Great Comebacks program to help people after surgery for colitis and to let everyone know that many people go on to do great things and live normal lives post-surgery.

> *"The surgery never held him back from doing anything,"* said
> Alberga.

As Dave laid in the hospital bed, Benirschke visited. Alberga's wife had convinced Rolf to go, worried about her husband.

> *"I had lost 50 pounds at this point in the hospital. And then one day, Benirschke walked in and said, 'What are you doing? What are you waiting for?' My fear was that I would be forced to live a normal life, and I did not want to live a normal life. I want to live an extraordinary life. Rolf convinced me that I could."*

Alberga went ahead and had the surgery, just in time.

> *"I was voted the closest to death in the hospital in 2000 without actually going over the edge. I was on a telemetry bed, with heart failure issues, and really it was almost too late."*

But make it he did, spending seven weeks in the hospital at one point. People reacted in different ways to his illness and recovery. As others who have faced life-changing events find, some friends who don't know how to handle it are driven away, while others draw closer.

> *"Some people were frightened by the whole thing,"* said Alberga. *"Some people I was close to never came to see me. Other people I hardly knew showed up every other day, and I've stayed close to them."*

The surgery was planned to take place in two stages. First, he had surgery to remove his colon and was sent home with a bag. Then, after he recovered, they planned for him to return six months later for a second surgery to build what is called a "J pouch," using tissues from his digestive system to create an internal space of live tissue to hold his waste.

Two weeks after the first surgery, Alberga went home extremely weak from the illness and procedure; this strengthened his resolve to work even harder to get back on his feet, get ready for the second surgery, and get on with his life.

> Alberga said, *"There were two steps into the living room and I was too weak to go up them. I was lying on my couch in a stupor from pain medication and thinking, 'Okay, I have to do this again in six months, I need to be ready.' I got up, got on the computer, and signed up for a triathlon in four and a half months. I could not even get into and out of bed alone. I had to go from weak, unable to support my own weight, to being ready for another major surgery in six months."*

For the triathlon, Alberga would have to run, swim, and bike, but for the first month after the surgery all he could do was walk, and even that was a struggle at first.

> *"A well-known triathlete friend would come over and walk with me. 'Come on, this time we'll walk all the way around the block,' she'd say. When alone, I'd walk in the dark, holding a pillow against my incision because I was afraid of what people would think."*

Once he was okay with the walking and recovering, he started swimming, going to the pool with his temporary ostomy bag by his side. For years he had worked hard to hide the fact that he had colitis, but when getting in the pool and going swimming, he could not hide things anymore. The bag would be obvious, out for anyone to see. But while he had worried for so long about revealing his condition, it was actually a good thing to finally get it out there. More than good even, it was great.

> *"I had to go in and out of the shower, in and out of locker room, and I was worried about what people would say. So I*

had to just go for it. People would ask about it, and I would just show them. For me, for the first time in my life I was able to be open about it. And it felt great. It was a huge relief, to just get it all out there. Yeah, it sucks but it's better than being dead."

One issue that made dealing with IBD hard, Alberga found, was that people seldom talk about it. While a heart attack is difficult to hide from your friends and colleagues, IBD is a topic that patients avoid talking about, afraid of shame and embarrassment. In my mind just the act of acknowledging and talking about such a topic helps more people accept it and deal with it, might even help more overcome it and find a cure.

While he had worried that people might think it weird or that his bag would make them shy away, the people Dave talked with about it were all supportive, to his surprise.

"The amazing thing was that the only comments I got were 'my grandma had one of those' or 'my mom had the same thing.' It's amazing how many people have gone through this or know someone who has."

And while he had worried about getting the surgery, thinking it would hold him back, this ended up not being a problem either.

"I scuba dived with the bag, raced with it, and I think I even went skydiving with it. I did the triathlon, and didn't set any records – but I did it. Then I called my doctor, and told him I was ready, and he scheduled me for the next week. We did the second surgery, and it set me back, but I was ready and recovered better than the first time. Overall, since the surgery I'm better. I'm cured, really."

His colitis behind him, and his business growing, Alberga has looked for ways he and the company could help solve important problems related to health and wellness for all of the great many people they reach – a natural fit for the business as well as for Alberga. The business of Active is focused on the intersection of people, activities, and events. Originally their business was primarily event registration for marathons and other races, but now they also serve parks around the country, sports leagues, corporate events, and organizations like the YMCA. Today, Active has more than 3,300 employees and 50,000 customers, the company processed more than 80 million transactions in 2011 alone, and Active Network went public in May 2011. Fulfilling its mission of connecting people with the activities they love, want, and need to do, Active's technology helps power participatory events for businesses and charities alike; its touch has reached over a third of all US households.

Because of Alberga's experience, fighting colitis is one way he's been giving back to the world. Having experienced colitis and how fitness helped him to overcome it, he's more committed than ever to helping others live the fullest lives they can.

> *"I wanted to leverage my role in Active and myself against health care in general. I joined the board of trustees of CCFA (Crohns and Colitis Foundation of America), which raises and grants over $20million per year for research and patient support. We combine fundraising with endurance events: training people to finish a seminal event in their life like a marathon in exchange for raising funds to help cure IBD. We will cure the disease. I'm convinced of it, and we're making a lot of progress."*

In addition to fighting colitis, Alberga has set his sights on an even larger health issue – the obesity epidemic.

"We have a health care time bomb. Two thirds of Americans are overweight, and this has only happened in the last fifteen to twenty years."

Dave started by looking for solutions that helped his teammates at Active Network, creating a program called Take a Load Off (TALO) to help them make healthier choices for themselves.

"TALO is all about changing fundamental behavior, about how you think about food and how you think about yourself," said Alberga. "It is not about the scale, or calorie counting. We teach people to read the back of the box and see if this is something they want to put in their body, building awareness of what they are eating. When you pause to think about what you are putting in your body, you can't help but reduce the calories you eat and eat better things. It's about educating people around a spectrum of choices."

Losing weight and getting fit is seldom easy, but it can be done, particularly with connections to others who want to help. More and more businesses are finding that it makes sense to provide this help, providing employees with creative programs like TALO that help them stay healthy and happy.

"As part of TALO, we have nutritionists and trainers on staff for employees, and we've just launched the second season, opening up registration for employees nationwide. About 25% of the people who participated in the first TALO program came out of it saying they were able to discontinue the use of medications they were on when the program started for treatment of conditions including diabetes and high blood pressure."

TALO targets those who are most at risk of obesity, and have the most to gain, but almost everyone wins by getting fitter, no matter where they stand today. Like Roger Wright in Chapter 4, the people at Active have found that making a commitment to others, making the project greater than yourself, and making it visible to your friends, family, and coworkers all boost the success rate. We might let a silent New Year's resolution fall quietly away, but a public commitment is something we stick with.

As part of the TALO program, Active holds an annual ActiveX Charity Challenge to raise money for local charities, while getting their employees to participate in a running event that fosters teambuilding and promotes fitness.

> *"For our ActiveX Charity Challenge, we have said that we will train you to run your first race, but you have to earn money for charity. Taking that a step further with TALO, we will take you from 12 weeks out, get you through the event, and you have to raise money. When you go out and ask your friends to support you, you've socialized your commitment. This effectively brings them into your support structure, and the likelihood that you'll drop out is much lower."*

The secret? Once again, the key to better lives and healthier lives is connecting with a greater good, taking on the challenge of building healthier lives by doing it for each other.

> *"We get better when we do it together,"* said Alberga. *"We make much greater progress toward better and healthier lives when we do it not just for ourselves but for our families, friends, and communities."* *This can work for fitness programs within other companies just as it has for Active Network with their own employees, and with so many other stories featured in this book. "I want to get to the stage where people will make a donation to a worthy charity in the name of a friend who has committed to stop smoking, or to quit eating*

> *fast food. This commitment mechanism can be applied to a bunch of other really healthy activities where you make a commitment in front of friends of families."*

If the program works at Active, they can make it work for others as well, delivering a fitness and wellness system other businesses can use to help employees anywhere.

> *"We're starting to roll out this program to individuals with our Active.com Trainer program, and we're also working to package it up and take it out to other companies. We're doing it now for Disney, and we just launched a similar program with Aetna and its health plan members. In a sense we are the crucible where we can test out these programs, then move them out to other companies. So far we haven't really failed with any one of the big programs. I'd say we've gotten more efficacy out of it than we expected."*

Active and Dave Alberga have the visibility, the commitment, and the tools to make change happen, and make it happen for lots of people, harnessing the power of committing to others and the power of a committed leader like Dave, who sees the potential for a business to be a catalyst for positive change. The results are still up to each person at the end of the day, but having help like this will allow more people to fight obesity or other health problems in their own lives.

It turns out this isn't bad for business either. While some still think that businesses have no place getting involved in the lives of those who work there, the great businesses are the ones who care – most importantly, who show it. One reason Active Network has been so successful is that those who work there believe in what they are doing, and know the business does too.

> *"I'm trying to do more than my part to have an impact, make a difference," said Alberga. "The legacy for the company is not*

just in the technology space, but a grander vision of trying to stem the tide in this epidemic. You jump out of bed every morning knowing how important this is, how exciting this work is for us."

People everywhere want work they can believe in, work they can be proud of for themselves and for their kids, work that makes a positive difference in the world. Active and Alberga provide a model for how this can be done.

Alberga's story is another exciting demonstration of the power we have to take our challenges then use them to propel us forward by connecting to a greater purpose. Alberga continues to give back by pushing his company to the nth degree in many ways. To help combat the nation's growing obesity epidemic, Alberga has Active Network participate in various lobbying efforts for government funding of health and wellness initiatives on Capitol Hill. Alberga also participates in a community-supported agriculture (CSA) program with a local organic farm to get his employees eating healthier. He has also implemented Active's highly successful ActiveX Employee Participation Program that includes more than 20 activities a week: walking/running groups, nutritional behavior workshops, smoking cessation, lunch yoga, nutritional seminars, and community volunteering.

Dave Alberga also hosts the ActiveX Charity Challenge, the company's yearly fund "racing" effort, where Active Network pays for the entry fee, training, and racing gear for all employees that raise a specified amount of money for a designated local charity. Last year, Active Network raised nearly $80,000 company-wide for local charities like Challenged Athletes Foundation and Girls on the Run. Active Network has raised over $250,000 for charities in the past three years.

When we finished our talk, Dave offered to go for a run together sometime. I might take him up on his offer sometime, even though I'm pretty sure he'll leave me in the dust.

Chapter 11: Finding a New Direction

Many of us deal with tragedy in our lives, but few of us face what **Crissy Saint** has. Crystal "Crissy" Saint was raised in Phoenix by her mom, who was in an abusive relationship, which was hard for a child to hide from. Many of us have parts of our life that we'd like to leave behind in the past; for Crissy, she remembers hiding in her room, hoping it would not be her.

Her aunt stepped in to take a young Crissy with her and raise her, making all the difference in Crissy's life. Her life was dramatically changed by this move and the warm, loving, and safe home her aunt provided for her to grow up in for many years. It was as if her aunt had given her a whole new life, and a far better one, with love, kindness, and respect. Crissy has remained immensely grateful to her aunt throughout her life for giving her this chance.

Not one to stand still for long, Crissy began working at an early age.

"I got my first job pretty much the week I turned 15. I was still in high school and as soon as I could work full-time, I did. I had school from 7:00 am to 3:00ish, soccer practice after that, and then would work 'til sometimes 2 or 3 in the morning. It was hard and when I got to college it didn't get easier. For a time I worked two full-time jobs and had 18 credit hours. I am not expecting a pity party or anything of the sort. Those were my circumstances and I had to do what I had to do."

The years passed and Crissy got a degree in psychology, got married, and found herself living in Phoenix, working for a major retailer in an office position. The job was okay, and she was glad to have a job at a time when many others didn't, but still in the back of her mind she felt it wasn't enough. More and more she came to realize that for all of the time she spent at work, her job was a paycheck but little more. Getting a paycheck was certainly a good thing – and nothing to sneeze at – but her job seemed to involve little more than moving papers, filling out forms, and checking boxes inside the corporate bureaucracy. With a degree in psychology, a deep passion for people, and an outgoing, creative spirit, she wanted to help people somehow, to do creative work that really connected her with others, but her job seemed to offer few opportunities to do this. Creativity was not encouraged in the corporate world she was immersed in.

Not happy, but not unhappy enough to make big changes, Crissy continued treading water with things as they were, even though she hated going to work each day. That is, until events in 2011 forced her hand.

On the morning of her five-year-old daughter's birthday, Crissy's aunt fainted in her home in Kansas City, Missouri. When taken to the hospital, they found that her aunt had advanced brain cancer. Treatment was undertaken immediately but the cancer was so advanced that there was little time and little hope.

> *"The doctors discovered multiple tumors in her brain and realized that they had already spread throughout the rest of her body. I struggled with the news and the shock of it all and flew out to Missouri with my partner to provide her with any support that I possibly could. When someone is on their last leg of life, you have no idea how hard it is to come up with the right words."*

We might have numerous friends and acquaintances, and some of us have large families, but most of us have a very small circle of people whom we hold closest in our hearts. Crissy's aunt was one of these people to her, one of those she held dearest in her life, and she felt helpless in the face of what was happening – there was little she could do or say, it seemed.

> *"I watched as her three-year-old boy and her little girl snuggled themselves in to her bosom as she lay in the hospital bed. Her head was bandaged up and large circles were drawn all over her forehead that marked where the radiation treatments should be concentrated. This wasn't fair. I remembered the times when I was a little girl and she would rescue me from a difficult childhood and let me know that I was loved. She was my heroine."*

Knowing the outlook was not good, her aunt put on a brave front for her family, even if they knew the truth of the situation.

> *"At times, during my short stay in Missouri, she would act as if this was a short hiccup in a long life. Stage 5 brain cancer? Pshh. Nothing. Yet, the silence in the room hung heavy on us like a damp wash cloth clinging to my face. At times I couldn't breathe, and I felt selfish when I actually could take in a breath because I knew that at some point in the not-so-distant future she would no longer be able to."*

Crissy returned home and her aunt was released from the hospital, but a short time after, in August 2011, Crissy got a call telling her that her aunt had passed away, only weeks after being diagnosed.

> *"Looking back, I realize the fight had left her long before my arrival in Missouri. I struggled with how a family could be devastated in such a way. I tried to push away my own pain,*

> *because at least I had gotten to know how beautiful a person she was. Her little ones would not get that chance."*

Crissy had few other family members she was close to. Her father had moved to Costa Rica 15 years earlier, and started a new family there. Her father's family in Costa Rica included a teenage girl, a half-sister to Crissy. Crissy had kept in contact with her father over the years, and then in recent years started traveling to Costa Rica when her job allowed, trying to rebuild their relationship, getting to know her father again, as well as his family. Her job only allowed limited time for travel though, and going to Costa Rica was a long trip.

Then Crissy got another call. It was September 29th when she woke up and saw that she had missed a call from Costa Rica.

> *"There was no voice mail so I didn't think much about it and I logged on to my computer. A few emails pop up from relatives I haven't seen in years telling me to call them – family emergency, they said. By that night I was on a plane and headed to the jungle. My father had shot himself early that morning and I didn't know what I was doing, but I knew I had to be there."*

Her father had struggled with terminal illness until he saw no end in sight, it seemed, and he had decided to end his life. When Crissy arrived, she found herself thrown up against the edge again by events outside of her control, and forced to be the source of strength for others.

> *"I struggled with my broken Spanish to understand the situation, the pain, and the loss felt by his fiancée and neighbors. I looked in to the eyes of the woman who he was set to marry in December and attempted to absorb as much pain from her as I possibly could and tuck it away somewhere for me to digest later."*

There were the practical difficulties of legal paperwork, lawyers, banks, and a language barrier for her to deal with. There was her half-sister she had only just started to know and the rest of her father's family in Costa Rica, who she felt a need to help. Crissy told herself to hold it together, for the time being at least, even as she found herself in a distant land dealing personally with the remains of her father.

> *"I was the eldest daughter, and wasn't it my role to figure this whole mess out? I looked over at my 14-year-old sister and realized that in all reality I barely knew her. The hardest part was at the morgue. We waited for hours on end to be able to see my father's body. Tradition in Costa Rica is to dress the dead. It's an honor, or a hell, and it's the family's duty. We walked in to the bare and curtained-off room in the basement and the pungent smell of death hit me like a putrid wall of the unknown. My father was wrapped up in a bloody sheet on a gurney off in the corner."*

> *"They don't embalm in Costa Rica and I wondered what to expect when the body was unwrapped. 'The body' is what it had become to me, because the reality that it was my father was too much to handle. We unwrapped him and I became a distant stranger in a sea of sobbing faces. I looked over at my young sister and said in broken Spanish to 'be strong.' It's what he would have said and I realized that she and I were the only ones not crying. I wondered if I was still human as we struggled to dress the body in my father's clothes."*

Returning home, Crissy's view of the world was rapidly shifting after the deaths of her father and her aunt. Life was short and she felt like she was letting hers slip away. Continuing with her old work, spending all of her days in something that felt meaningless: it seemed like this was no longer an option. Something had to give.

"On a layover flight from L.A., I had the wonderful experience of sitting next to a guy who had recently quit working on something he had built his entire career up to. While I won't disclose the details, I can say it was a major film production. Yet he realized that he was just completely miserable and that the job just wasn't worth sacrificing his happiness over. When he told me his story, I was in awe. He had done exactly what I had been wanting to do for years. He had done exactly what millions of Americans are probably wanting to do right now. I am not advocating walking the plank if the job you currently have is fulfilling – those jobs are rare and are priceless – what I'm saying is that it's smart to think about your level of happiness at your current job and explore the possibilities of being happier. You are worth that, aren't you?"

Leaving her job was not easy for Crissy. She'd worked all her life, never skipping a beat. She was not one to complain, and would not have given the idea of quitting a thought normally. But it was time for a change. More than time, really. She enjoyed the people she worked with and had grown close to them after eight years at her job. But it wasn't enough. For years she had thought that there was no other way, but she now saw that this wasn't true.

"There are trillions of options in the world – why waste a life at one that does not fulfill you, challenge you, and allow you to be the happy person you are meant to be? I am an intelligent person who has a passion and zest for life that is sometimes overwhelming. I realized that I am worth more. It is important to realize that every hour you spend at your job should truly be worth giving up. My hours were not. At some point, the trade became unbalanced."

So she took the plunge, diving into a new future, even if wasn't sure what that future would look like. Having faced the death of those close to her, her view on life was changed. What felt important to her, or not important, had shifted dramatically. She started thinking beyond just paying the bills to think about what she really wanted out of life.

> *"After not being satisfied with my job for a few years now, I finally put in my two weeks notice. A lot of people are bound to give me grief when they find out that I haven't secured a replacement job yet. I expect it. Most people can't imagine what their lives would be without a job. Fear is a natural emotion that helps us to survive. The thing is, though, that I am done just 'surviving.'*

> *"I remind myself how very short life is – how shorter it can unexpectedly become – and then I ponder how I am spending my day. Is it what I want to be doing? Lately, the answer to that question has been a big, fat no. That needs to change."*

Looking for a new job she would really believe in, Crissy started working with Gangplank, a non-profit collaborative work space with a focus on community, and the opening of a new location of theirs in Avondale, Arizona, in West Phoenix. Gangplank gives entrepreneurs and would-be entrepreneurs the infrastructure they need to get their ideas off the ground, helping them to turn their dreams into a viable business. The people she works with there are creative, thoughtful, and daring, like she is. Working at Gangplank, and working with people like this, is a huge and rewarding change for Crissy – just the kind of thing she was looking for when she took the leap into the unknown. She took a risk, and the world helped her out.

In addition to Gangplank, Crissy is also working at the MM Identity Lab as a social media and communications strategist. Located in a refurbished warehouse, MM Identity Lab is another creative and collaborative environment where she feels she can finally engage her inner needs, growing in exciting new directions. She said, "By the grace of God, it's another place where the same mentality holds. It's the most creative space you can imagine."

For years she kept putting off change, just getting by, until the world gave her a big push with some hard events that reminded her how short and precious life is: no day is to be wasted.

> *"These sorts of events make a person step away from all of the hustle and bustle of everyday life that we all get caught up in and take a look at the bigger picture. They help us to step away and ask questions like: Am I happy with my job? Am I spending enough time with my family? Do I wake up every morning and dread the day ahead of me?"*

All of this for Crissy is a part of turning over a new leaf, of taking what has happened to her as a key moment to move in a new and better direction. And by getting involved in creative work like Gangplank and helping others, she's already finding it is helping her to get her own life moving and growing.

> *"I would love to someday start a collaborative work space elsewhere in the nation with a huge emphasis on helping educate teens and kids on their work options and how to be entrepreneurs. I am extremely interested in community building events and helping people to see the options that exist out there for healthy and happy work options. I'm giving back and connecting with people on more of larger scale. A lot of crappy things happen, but I keep moving, keep growing, and putting a positive vibe out in the world."*

We might not always have control over the things that happen to us, but we do have control over how we respond to them. Sometimes it feels like the world is sending us a message, telling us that it's time to take a look at our lives and see if we like where we're going – that it's time to make a change for the better, to spend our time doing things we care about, things that matter. The message may not be an easy one, and might shake us to our core, but if we're able to listen, the result can be phenomenal.

To get in contact with Crissy: www.crissysaint.wordpress.com/

Chapter 12: Overcoming Cancer and Divorce

You would think that having one big trauma in your life would be enough, but after **Christine Clifford** beat breast cancer 18 years ago she went on to go through two painful divorces. She found the strength to face all of this by taking these bad things and finding the good in the hard-won but valuable lessons that come through experience. One of the good things she has learned is the value of humor along with empathy in dealing with painful problems like cancer or divorce. Humor helps us put things in perspective, letting go of the pain and fear; it helps us see that life is bigger than our problems.

Christine was 40 years old when she was diagnosed with breast cancer. Breast cancer remains a significant and intense medical challenge, but it was even harder on patients 18 years ago when Christine was originally diagnosed: for many patients, the treatments seemed worse than the disease. Christine herself went through ten months of high-dose chemotherapy delivered every two weeks, and 33 days of radiation therapy.

> *"I lost my hair, but I was only 40 and thank god I was fit, and resilient,"* said Christine. *"I've been cancer-free ever since."*

It was not a path Christine chose for herself, but when her life took her in this direction she emerged with a new perspective. Rather than getting stopped in her tracks, she found a fresh way to see the world. And early on, she realized that simple survival was not an option; her new lease on life gave her a new sense of pride, strength, and hope.

> *"I learned from my cancer experience that we're stronger than we think we are, and that there are so many more people that want to provide us support and encouragement than we ever knew existed. And the biggest lesson was that every day of my life is a gift. Every day I'm grateful for the sun shining, for 18 years of life I never expected to have."*

Having learned so much, and knowing that there are more people all the time struggling to deal with cancer, she founded The Cancer Club in 1995. Christine found a way to turn her experience into a way to help others, to move forward in her life with a new sense of purpose.

> *"We've helped thousands of people find hope, inspiration, and humor in their own cancer journeys. I have also raised over $1,000,000 for breast cancer research through my own celebrity golf tournament."*

One way that The Cancer Club helps is with the latest information about developments in chemotherapy or ways that women can improve their overall health. Another important message that Christine delivers in her lectures is that there is life after dealing with cancer, and a good life at that.

It's important that cancer patients hold on to hope, keeping a better future bright in their minds. But it's not all serious business. Cancer often makes those near the cancer patient so fearful and uncomfortable that it hurts their social and personal connections, which the patient needs most at this time. Many people back away from the cancer patient, afraid perhaps that the illness or just the thought of it will reach their own lives somehow. Cancer is a serious thing, but maybe we're too serious about it if we allow fear to take over the life of the patient. Christine has found that humor is a great tool to change this. Even in cancer there is something to laugh about, and by laughing at it we can dispel the fear; get back to fighting and winning against cancer, and building a life beyond it.

> *"Humor is a great connector of people,"* said Christine. *"I needed people in my life, but what I found was that when someone found I had cancer, they did not know what to say and were afraid of saying the wrong thing, so they often did not speak to me. So I use humor to put them at ease, and then the floodgate opens."*

Christine includes humor in the talks she gives, but has also created books with funny cartoons for patients, including her first book which was called "*Not Now, I'm Having a No Hair Day*".

> *"When I was diagnosed with cancer, people would do silent gestures of support, sending flowers or a card, or ring my doorbell, but they would not have face-to-face interactions. What I started doing was to draw cartoons for thank you notes. I drew a cartoon of a son yelling up the stairs 'Mom, more flowers for your breast.' Then someone would pick up the phone and call me, and then the dialogue started."*

Christine found that in addition to humor, having a regular exercise routine helped her to heal and recover.

> *"What saved me was that I'm an avid exerciser, walking four miles a day, six days a week."*

This point, the value of exercise, came up with many of the people I spoke with, including Mark, Roger, Alyssa, and Dave. Our mind and body work together, and exercise seems to improve not just our physical condition but our optimism and feeling of empowerment, improving our ability to heal.

Having been through cancer, Clifford has also found that the need to give back and help others became an important part of her life.

> *"Cancer patients want to help others, maybe creating a product or service, or raising money for research. A lot of people who survive adversity want to give back. They have the 'There but for the grace of god' feeling, asking themselves, 'Why did I survive?' And, I think, they instinctively feel the value of being grateful and helping others as part of their own healing process, becoming whole."*

The next great challenge in Christine's life came in a completely different form. We hope that we can trust and rely on those we know, love, and marry; it can be a crushing blow when we find we can't. Christine had married her college sweetheart and was married for 29 years, but then found he had committed what she calls "financial infidelity."

> *"My first husband ran up a $100,000 line of credit without telling me that came due. This was after I had supported him for our entire marriage."*

This was the end of the relationship road for her – a line that had been crossed, a trust that had been betrayed.

> *"My first divorce was very difficult and still is hard to think about. Fortunately, we're still friends."*

She filed for divorce and moved on.

Perhaps she did not move on far enough, though; it seems she went out of the frying pan and into the fire, with another lesson to be learned the hard way.

> *"I quickly rebounded with what ended up being a violent, severely alcoholic, diagnosed sociopath, who lied to me about his finances. He was almost a million dollars in debt*

> *when I married him. He hadn't paid his taxes in three years. One of his ex-wives sued him for $400,000 in unpaid child support and alimony. His Mercedes got repossessed right out of our parking garage. He hadn't paid his bills."*

If Christine thought it couldn't get worse after her first divorce, she quickly learned she was wrong.

> *"After suffering through domestic abuse for almost four years, I got the courage to leave, even though I had been left almost financially bankrupt by the two marriages."*

This was a very hard lesson to learn, but she was not alone, she quickly realized. Millions of women go through the trauma of divorce, and feel alone, left on their own to deal with seemingly overwhelming problems. These millions of women need help, starting with their finances, among many other things. Turning her problem into an opportunity to help other women going through the same hard times she had, she decided to deliver help for these women by creating Divorcing Divas in April 2010. Divorcing Divas hosts all-day educational conferences for people going through divorce, including keynote speakers, vendors from college education to handymen, even sex toy vendors to home-based business advisors. Resources that single women might want to find in their life. Handling her events professionally, Christine and Divorcing Divas attract big-name sponsors like Merrill Lynch, Bremer Bank, and UBS Financial, to name a few, as well as other experts that the recently divorced need, all in one place to help them get back on their feet and moving on with the next chapter in their life.

The difficult economic times we've been through of late have put a lot of strains on marriages, Christine has found.

> *"I have definitely seen a huge surge in people who have turned to Divorcing Divas for advice on their financial*

> *situation. Many people, men and women, would really like to*
> *initiate a divorce, but feel the strains of the economy are*
> *holding them back. My approach is to always steer them to a*
> *financial advisor who can help them make educated*
> *decisions."*

Christine has found that humor helps people deal with divorce much the same as it does with cancer. She again wrote a book based on her own experiences, entitled *"The Clue Phone's Ringing... It's for You! Healing Humor for Women Divorcing."*

When Christine does events and talks with people, they remind her how important her help is for some.

> *"The work has given me new meaning in life, and the lives*
> *I've touched through my conferences have been amazing.*
> *One of our attendees wrote on her evaluation, 'When I arrived*
> *at your conference this morning, I was petrified with fear. I*
> *am leaving this afternoon knowing that your event saved my*
> *life.' That's how scared a lot of people are; whatever the*
> *adversity is, they are scared to death. If they can be*
> *educated, see someone who has moved forward, then they*
> *can do that too."*

Through her business Christine also raises money for women who need help and have few other options to overcome problems like domestic violence.

> *"Part of the mission of Divorcing Divas is to raise money for*
> *Tubman, one of the first non-profit women's shelters in the*
> *country for abused women."*

Not finding what she needed in her life, Christine created a new life for herself: she provides a model for the great many others who are seeking a new life after going through cancer or divorce. She shows via example that great things are still to come, regardless of the problems we face today.

> "People come to me because they want to know if they can have a new life. And I like to think I'm a great example of someone who has persevered, so they can do it, too. I didn't really have anyone to go to who could show me the way – either with cancer, because I was so young, or divorce, so I decided that is what I wanted to do: show others, by example, that they can move forward and find an even better life than the one they had before."

> "Life after adversity is all about rebuilding: relationships, attitude, finances, the purpose of your life. I have an overwhelming feeling of gratitude – every single day – that I've seen my two little boys, who were 10 and 8 when I was diagnosed with cancer, graduate from high school, then college, and now out in the work force. I am grateful that I found the courage to leave my second marriage. It wasn't easy either. So I always ask myself at the end of the day, 'What was I meant to learn from that experience?'"

Looking forward, Christine is still learning and still thinking of ways to expand her work to reach more people. Living in Minneapolis, she's focused her efforts there, but there's a whole world of people facing challenges (like cancer and divorce) who need help. Christine is looking at ways to bring her events to other cities in order to reach this larger group.

When she got started, Christine was the one who needed help – when she couldn't find what she needed she got into action to create the help, knowing many others must go through the same thing as her. These were "up against the wall"-type events, and there's no telling what might have happened, but when there was a demand she started inventing, and not just for herself but for all the others who need help as well. In hindsight, having gone through what she did and accomplished all she has as a result, she wouldn't change a thing.

> *"I'm confident I would never have started my own companies and written books about my experience if I hadn't been diagnosed with breast cancer and gone through two very difficult divorces," said Christine. "I actually look at these adversities as the gifts in my life. They renewed my faith, strengthened my bonds with family and friends, and gave me permission to do creative things like speaking, my books, and starting companies; things I never would have thought of doing in a million years. They changed my life so profoundly – for the better – that I would never go back and change what happened to me."*

> *"Today I have come to a place in my life where I feel totally fulfilled. It's a place I've always aspired to reach," said Christine. "And I realize that the path to pleasure has been through pain. It's all about the risks I've taken in my life. I've always been a person who took risks, and now I realize that the best parts of my life have come from the biggest risks I have taken. When I was diagnosed and started The Cancer Club, I left my job with salary, bonuses, and commissions, following a dream to help cancer patients. The risk I took was immeasurable. Everyone has challenges in their life: diseases, loss of jobs and homes, the death of loved ones, environmental catastrophes. But the resilience of the human spirit is amazing. I am hoping that perhaps I've had my fill of the 'bad stuff' and now, I look for the good."*

Christine's story reveals again that every challenge holds a lesson; further, that sometimes the hardest experiences hold the most valuable lessons if we are willing to see them and grow with them as well. Such struggles as cancer and divorce are scary, forcing us to rethink our lives. Hope for a better future is a powerful tool, along with humor, information, and help from others. If you are experiencing cancer or divorce, or know someone who is, they might benefit from the work Christine is doing. She is an example of someone who has been through hard times and not only survived, but turned her greatest challenges around to build a bright, new, beautiful life.

More resources: www.cancerclub.com

www.divorcingdivas.com

Chapter 13: Fighting the Odds and Winning

A physician's assistant in Atlanta, **Alyssa Phillips** was known to all of her friends as a real health nut, and she deserved the title. She worked hard for it, running six miles every morning before surgery; at age 31, she had never felt better. But Alyssa had started losing weight without even trying, and she soon found out why. Just weeks after running her best time ever in a half-marathon, she was told during a visit to her gynecologist that she had a rare and aggressive form of cervical cancer, with a tumor that had already grown to more than 4 cm in size and had spread to her liver, resulting in multiple tumors there as well.

Cancer is always scary, and this was not your average cancer. Fighting cancer starts with identifying it, but Alyssa's cancer was so unusual that her doctors struggled to figure out what exactly they were dealing with, even as the cancer continued growing rapidly in her body. Within a few days, a pathologist at a nationally-recognized hospital acknowledged that she was one of only a handful of women to ever be diagnosed with "Large-Cell Neuroendocrine Cancer of the Cervix…with Distant Metastases."

The prognosis was not good. Her doctors told her she had only a 5% chance of living. Happily married to the love of her life, Alyssa and her husband had been hoping to have kids – that was now out of the question.

"I very quickly began to understand that I had instantly gone from being in the prime of my life to being in the fight of my

life, facing my own mortality suddenly and squarely in the face," said Alyssa.

Her cancer was so unusual that there was little information available about it, but by what she says are divine circumstances she found an expert oncologist who put together a medical plan to fight it, and Alyssa started putting together an internal plan to fight it as well.

"I was terrified because things seemed to be going from horrible to hopeless faster than I could process them," wrote Alyssa about the experience. *"But as they told me and everyone else in my life was falling apart, knowing that I had basically just been given a death sentence, I exhaled for the first time since this nightmare had begun. We had a name. And that also meant that we could now have a plan. Game on."*

The plan started with a radical hysterectomy just six days after her initial doctor visit, followed rapidly by aggressive chemotherapy to force the liver tumors back into remission. This was then to be followed by two rounds of chemotherapy high enough to kill any remaining cancer cells in her body; the drawback was that it would kill her immune system as well, and require a bone marrow transplant to rebuild her immune system afterward. Moreover, the plan was to do the high dose chemo and bone marrow transplant not once but twice. With her immune system stripped down to nothing, she would then need to spend almost a year in closely controlled surroundings to prevent any infections, which could have been lethal in her vulnerable state.

"They were literally going to strip me down to my elemental beginnings and press the restart button –twice," wrote Alyssa. *"Oh, and then 'hope for the best.' Awesome, where do I sign up?"*

It was a long shot, but it was her best shot at making it through.

"As you know, we don't have many cases like yours to compare to, but we've tried this treatment on about four other patients and three are doing well," her doctor told her. They didn't have to tell her what happened to the fourth patient. She already knew and Alyssa was determined not to have the same fate. She would be the 4th patient to live through this treatment and be cured. For her, there was no other option.

Alyssa's family had been through tragedy when her sister died while they were in college. They had been close, and she was devastated when her sister quickly succumbed to bacterial meningitis. She had thought that a person would not have to go through something this difficult more than once in their life. As her condition became clear, she realized she had been wrong, but she was determined this time to come out on top.

Somewhere in the midst of this swirl of confusing and frightening events, Alyssa made a crucial decision – the kind that makes all the difference. She decided she had to live, and she knew instinctively that hope was an essential part of this. She did what she could to help her body (along with her doctors). Above all she knew that her heart and her mind were her own and this was where the real fight would be. She knew she had to keep the flame of hope alive, to get through it all and build a new life for herself, to give herself the chance to do the great things she still had ahead of her.

> *"I won't lie – it was tough. Really tough,"* wrote Alyssa. *"And not so much the treatments, although those were no cake walk, but it was the restart button that was pressed inside of me, which somehow happened alongside the physical one, that was the real challenge. Facing my own mortality in complete isolation, while staring death squarely in the face*

and gritting my teeth with a firm 'No;' stirring myself up over and over again to stay positive when everything else around me was dragging me in the opposite direction; staying laser-focused on what I wanted and not on what was actually happening...now that was hard."

Alyssa's first bone marrow transplant was in November of 2008, and the second was near Christmas, only five weeks later. Then she spent long months allowing her immune system to rebuild, carefully tending to her body.

"I bided my time for several more months of house arrest by continuing all of my newly-learned disciplines: having to get extra creative with food preparation since I could only eat cooked items; showering with Press-and-Seal, ziplock baggies, and duct tape to protect the catheter still embedded in my chest from the treatments, and chose to look at this time of isolation as a rare opportunity to press the pause button in life rather than being just locked away from the world while we waited."

By the time spring came, Alyssa's hair was starting to grow back and her doctors cleared her to go outside. She had to get accustomed to the world again after being hidden away and get used being outside again, exercising regularly.

"Having been absent for so long, the world seemed strange and loud and busy now," wrote Alyssa. *"It was as if I had emerged from a dark cave after a long hibernation and was squinting in the blazing light and noise of the world. It took me a while to get my legs back under me, so to speak. My physical body made a pretty miraculous comeback – I was running again just two months after my last transplant and I had power-walked on the treadmill of the bone marrow unit*

(and at home) every day during my treatments and beyond. The inside took a bit longer to heal. Actually, a lot longer."

As she continued growing stronger so did her hope; Alyssa forced herself to believe that she had made it. She had beaten the odds and survived. Her doctors continued watching her closely, and they still check on her periodically, but her body was cancer-free, and she had been given a new life. And then, in true form, Alyssa made another big decision. Surviving wasn't enough – she decided to do something great with this new life she'd been given, to live with a new larger purpose in life.

Like others, Alyssa got to a place where she saw all that had happened – as difficult as it had been – as a gift, opening new doors that she never would have opened before on her own.

> *"I would help other people with what I'd been through," Alyssa recalled realizing. "I realized again that I couldn't change some of the things that had happened, but I could choose how I looked at them and what I did with it. I could either choose to sit there and feel sorry for myself or I could get busy living this amazing second chance at life that I'd been given. We all get to choose what we do with our lives and I'm determined to choose well because I was given a clean slate. I'd been shattered into a million, irreparable pieces by what happened and I'd had to rebuild, starting over from the ground up, in every sense. I was new, inside and out. And I think that's the whole point. You see, I had to let go of the life I'd always assumed I'd live to allow this new one to emerge. So there was a death. It just wasn't the one everyone expected, and it was no less real to me."*

Alyssa has moved on to start working with charities that help patients, educating patients and doctors about this rare form of cancer and the cutting-edge treatment protocol she received. She also consults with people to share the critical tools she used and is working to share her story with more people to give them the gift of the hope that carried her through the darkest of times.

> *"This has always been bigger than me. Even from the start I knew if I could just make it through to the other side that it would then be my mission to share all that I learned and was led to. At the core of my motivation for what I'm doing now I want to give others the life-changing perspective I gained from leaning over the edge that separates this life and the next without having to go through what I did to learn it! In the end, I feel blessed. Most people say they don't know what their true purpose is, what they alone came here to do. I know exactly what mine is now, because there is every reason for me not to be here."*

People facing cancer or other great challenges may not see any light at the end of the tunnel, and feel their hope slipping away. Seeing someone like Alyssa who's made it makes all the difference, showing them it can be done. And by telling them the details of how she did it, mentally and physically, she can help them do the same.

> *"I am focused full-time on sharing my message now. I feel called to share it and all I've learned. I was so desperate for this information and even just to know that someone else had made it. Everyone has a story. Everyone's been through challenges, and when people hear my story it just drops all the walls and they share theirs with me, like, 'Oh, she gets it. She's been there. She knows.' I love that. It's such an incredible honor to have others share their lives with me."*

For herself, and for so many others, Alyssa has seen firsthand the power of hope to make all the difference, no matter what the odds are.   If there was one thing she could tell people, Alyssa says it would be to keep hoping, regardless of how bad things look, regardless of statistics or expert opinions.

> *"Don't ever let anyone steal your hope.   Hope, faith, and belief are so, so important. Critical even. A lot of people talk about this but I can't stress enough what a 'difference maker' they are. Your heart and your mind are your most powerful tools in this fight, and you have sole control over them. Use them, use everything you have. [Hope] is real and it can change the course of your life. Everyone's life."*

> *"We're all facing our mortality all the time," said Alyssa, reflecting on her story and the path ahead for her. "So the question becomes, what are you going to do with your life, your challenges, your tragedies? I choose to be better for them and to use them for good. In the end, you have to believe. You have to stretch beyond what's before you and reach for something higher."*

Alyssa blows me away with this amazing story that shows me yet again how much more we are capable of, if we only believe. She's been to a dark place, where few have been, and from where even fewer have returned, but she refused to give up no matter how awful things appeared. Hope can be inspired by many things around us in our lives, but ultimately hope comes from within us. By keeping our hope alive, we keep ourselves alive. By believing in something greater, we become something greater.

I can't wait to see what else Alyssa has in store. She is cancer-free, and I've got a feeling that she has more amazement still up her sleeves. She's working on a book about her experiences, describing how others can win their own struggle with cancer; after seeing all she has to stay, I know that the book will be phenomenal.

You can find out more about events, the book, and everything else Alyssa is working on at her website, www.alyssaphillipsinc.com. Stay tuned.

Chapter 14: Harnessing the Greater Good

 Doubt is unavoidable in life, no matter how hard we try. I know I've had times when I was filled with doubt, without a clue about which way to go, times when I'd go to great lengths to squelch the anxiety that stems from doubt. Doubt can be extremely uncomfortable, which might be why we try so hard to avoid it, but it turns out there are two kinds of doubt. There are healthy doubts that help guide us in making good choices and there are also unhealthy doubts stemming from irrational fears that can block our path through life, leading us into endless detours. Those with obsessive compulsive disorder (OCD) struggle constantly with these unhealthy doubts, to such an extent that these doubts can take over their lives.

Jeff Bell struggled with crippling OCD for many years. On the radio in the afternoons doing news in the San Francisco area, Bell speaks with a smooth clear voice perfect for radio, devoid of hesitation. Being on live radio has helped his progress with OCD, forcing him for at least that part of the day to focus on the present rather than dwelling on doubts of the past or future. Hearing him on the radio, you might not know the turmoil that has plagued him inside.

When driving, Bell would stop when he hit a pothole: his doubts would be telling him he may have hit someone, telling him he needed to go back, check and see. Relenting to the voice of doubt, he would stop, go back, check, and then go on. And then go back to check again. And then check again. Fearing he would hit another car, he was afraid to drive. He knew these worries did not make sense, but knowing this did not seem to help. He had undergone therapy, but nothing seemed to provide much relief, leaving him trapped by his own responses to the world around him. He found himself exhausted, at the end of his rope, stopped at every turn by his condition.

> *"During my worst years, I could barely leave the house because of my OCD,"* said Bell. *"I gave up driving, and relied on my wife to hold our family together. I considered quitting my job and giving up on ever living a normal life. My world was very dark for many years."*

> Finally, staring up at the stars one night, Bell told the universe, *"Show me how to turn around this crazy life, and I'll share my story with anyone who will listen."*

He waited but there was no cosmic message beamed back in his direction, so he took matters into his own hands and starting telling his story. Somehow he must have instinctively known that by reaching outside of himself to help others, he would also end up aiding himself. Over the process of writing two books and talking to people everywhere, helping them with their own challenges, Jeff gained control over his own symptoms.

Bell found the solution to his problems by taking a step back from his OCD, forcing himself to rethink the patterns and choices he would make. The solution came when he saw that there was a world that needed and relied on him to make good choices: to get out of unproductive patterns and decisions not just for himself, but for others as well.

To help me understand where he was coming from, Bell first explained OCD to me.

> *"OCD is known as the doubting disease,"* said Bell. *"At the core of OCD is this 'What if' question – what if I didn't wash*

my hands? What if I didn't turn off the iron? It's a biological disorder, with OCD sufferers locked in their brain and taking ridiculous measures to prevent uncertainty."

We all have uncertainty in life and doubts about which way to go – OCD sufferers included. For every move we make there is a good choice and a bad choice, even for countless small decisions we make each day, often without thinking about it. But these choices get switched around for those with OCD, making even the small choices hard to navigate.

"When you have OCD and suffer these doubts, your good and bad choices get very twisted," said Bell. *"If I have to go through a door to go somewhere, going to work or to school, the good choice for most people is to open the door and go through. With OCD, though, if I'm afraid of germs and think the door handle has germs on it, OCD says the good choice is not to open the door, but to stay away from the door because this reduces anxiety. The good choice and bad choice are backwards."*

The choices become oriented around compulsions that (temporarily at least) reduce the sky-high anxiety levels those affected feel because of their doubts. In this, OCD sufferers are not alone. For many of us our decisions become oriented around reducing anxiety rather than producing the best long-term result for us, those around us, and the greater world. Bell describes a way out of this:

"There is another choice though, and not one we usually think of: the 'greater good choice,' one that is bigger than me and my doubts. I had to learn that by making a greater good choice, by acting beyond my worry about germs, I would have a larger reward. I had to connect with a greater sense of purpose or service to somebody else."

The greater good choice can be found almost anywhere, in decisions large and small.

> *"Let's say I am a school teacher, for example, and I can't get to class on time because I can't get through doorways; I'm standing outside the door and unable to open it because of my OCD germ concerns. My good choice and my bad choice are backwards, but the greater good choice is to get into classroom and help the kids to learn."*

As Bell saw how this worked and used it more and more in his own life, his OCD got more and more under control. And the greater good for Bell came through his work helping others with OCD to do the same.

> *"My OCD recovery began in earnest when I decided to share my story in hopes of helping others with OCD. I developed the Greater Good Perspective Shift that allowed me to willfully choose between the perceived 'good' of indulging my compulsions and the 'Greater Good' of choosing, instead, to find ways to be of service to others and, in so doing, build my own sense of purpose. This motivation model continues to serve as the core of my outreach in the OCD community."*

> *"While traditional [exposure] therapy was a major part of my OCD recovery, the 'Greater Good' motivation my outreach affords me has really made all the difference,"* said Bell. *"There is something powerful about reaching out to help others this way, something science is beginning to understand is real. The reason we started saying 'a greater good' is that the good choice seems safe, but a greater good choice is even more powerful, enhancing our sense of purpose."*

Once Bell saw how powerful the Greater Good perspective was in his own life and for other OCD sufferers, he realized it was really much bigger than OCD. Thinking of the greater good can help people facing any number of life challenges to get up, dust themselves off, and start doing great things for others and themselves. It might seem backward at first for people who are hurting to spend their time and energy helping others, but in fact it might be just what people need as part of their own recovery. It might even be the key to your own problems you're dealing with right now.

> *"What we found was using this applies to people without OCD, those dealing with uncertainty in general – and all of us dealing with adversity are dealing with uncertainty,"* said Bell. *"When you have a big problem you're dealing with there's a great deal that is unknown about the future. People get their good and bad choices turned around. If you have cancer, for example, it might seem that the good choice is simply to shut down and isolate yourself. But if you push through the discomfort to the greater good by helping others around you, you not only help others who are in need – you also empower yourself."*

> *"Victor Frankl, the Holocaust survivor, was a psychiatrist who had his life's work, a textbook he was working on, confiscated,"* Bell told me. *"He spent years in the [concentration] camps recreating the book on slips of paper. He found that, among those not killed by camp guards, the major difference between survivors and non-survivors was that survivors had a specific purpose driving them. As Frankl discovered, our single greatest motivator is our search for a sense of purpose and meaning."*

> *"In the search for advocacy, you shift your thinking from victimization and thinking over and over, 'Why do I have this?'*

to thinking of opportunities to help people out. There's some exciting, fascinating science around this concept being done at UC Berkeley's Greater Good Science Center, where the study of the power of service, altruism, and compassion, once considered to be very soft science, is now very mainstream. Some of these studies suggest there's not only a psychological benefit associated with these practices, but also one connected with brain chemicals and the responses of the nervous system."

Seeing that the power of working for the greater good was so much bigger than himself and even larger than OCD, Bell cofounded an organization with Patti Lowery, creating a way to reach more people ready to turn their own adversity into advocacy.

"I recently launched a non-profit organization called The Adversity 2 Advocacy Alliance (A2A), aiming to showcase the power of turning one's personal challenges into service for others with similar challenges: cancer survivors helping other cancer survivors, recovering alcoholics helping other recovering alcoholics, and more. The project grew out of my own 'A2A' transformation, but now includes dozens of amazing individuals who have transformed their lives through targeted service. We recently put out 'A Call for A2A Stories' and are already hearing from remarkable folks across the country."

The people working through the A2A Alliance are as varied as their causes, including people like Corey Reich and Mary Nicholson. After falling down a set of stairs while at college, Corey was diagnosed with ALS, often called Lou Gehrig's disease. A2A helped Corey spread the word about his "Corey's Crusade" project, which has raised over $1.5 million for ALS research so far. Meanwhile, Mary Nicholson suffered a stroke soon after losing her husband to cancer. Finding her way back through therapy and a support group, she soon found herself helping other stroke sufferers as well, and founding the non-profit Healings in Motion.

These are just two of the incredible and inspiring stories that Jeff Bell and The A2A Alliance have encountered as they reach out to people dealing with a wide range of challenges, helping them turn their own challenges into new lives and new opportunities filled with purpose. The organization accepts donations at their site, and they are always eager to hear your story as well, even working with journalists who can often help you to tell your story, reach out to others, and reach for a better life yourself.

In our search for purpose and healing in our own lives, it is always inspiring to see how others have overcome their challenges, and even more exciting when they have discovered simple steps we can all take with the problems that we face. Jeff Bell's story is far larger than himself and it's a great example of what we can do. To learn more about his story of learning to manage his OCD and harness the power of choosing the greater good, his books are a phenomenal resource. His first book, *"Rewind, Replay, Repeat"*, is his personal memoir of coming to terms with OCD and his demons of doubt. Bell's second book, *"When in Doubt, Make Belief"*, is a crystal-clear exploration of doubt, the world inside OCD, and how belief can be conjured and crafted to hold back OCD – or, how all of us can deal with our unhealthy doubts by harnessing the power of belief.

You can read more about A2A and their work at www.adversity2advocacy.org

New Beginnings

The other day I went back again for a walk down by the creek in a nearby canyon. It was Spring, and although it doesn't usually rain much here in Southern California, it had rained heavily the day before so that the small creek was running high and the trail was muddy. I stopped and watched the water, listening to it softly murmur as it ran quickly downstream through the trees and brush. It was cold out, the trees shuddering and whispering in the wind. It felt good to get out.

Sometimes wildfires sweep through this area, but at the time the surrounding hills were covered in waves of shimmering, lush grass. The last time there was a fire, a few years before, the hills nearby were dark and charred at first, but the vegetation quickly recovered. I've heard some plants have seeds that will only sprout after they've been through a fire that scorches their outer shell, allowing the seed inside to get water and sprout. Maybe that's the way we are too, built like those seeds. Sometimes we grow best after we get burned a bit.

I stopped and watched the surface of the creek shimmer, reflecting the trees and the sky. Picking a stem from a tall stalk of grass, I ran the tasseled seeds through my fingers and thought of all the people I've talked with, like Mark running all the way to a new life after his heart transplant, Alyssa overcoming her cancer against all odds, and Jeff overcoming his OCD by working for the greater good. Some who I've talked with are far down the path of recovery and others are still finding their way. All of them are embarking on a brave new path in their life journey, letting go of their old life and reaching for something new. Passing through the fire, they discovered a whole new world of vast possibility waiting on the other side.

These people went through some rough times but they survived, and having survived they made a decision to set out to create a new life, one filled with purpose. None of them could say for sure where exactly their life's path would lead, but having passed through the fire they knew they had far to go still, and that what had seemed like a tragedy was actually a great gift – the gift of a second chance that could be filled with a new purpose.

This is the part that really got my attention. As different as all of these people are, they all found the same thing: no matter what they had been through, they had an amazing new life ahead filled with the purpose of reaching out beyond their own lives to help others in the world around them.

As amazing as the people in this book are, they're not alone. We might not all have the benefit of the spiritual shock treatment these people went through, and we probably would never go out looking for something like this, but we can all decide to start anew. We can still our inner demons, and see the world with clear fresh eyes, each and every one of us. We can follow those who've been to the edge and back, then learn from them, finding our way to the same conclusions they've reached to give ourselves a fresh start.

This probably sounds like a tall order, but it might be easier than you think. We have a deep instinct that drives us to seek a purpose in life, something we can get excited to be a part of every day when we wake up in the morning, whether the sun is shining or not. Just getting by isn't enough, no matter how hard we work to convince ourselves that it is. We want more. We need more. Finding our purpose is one of humanity's endless searches. We forget sometimes – we get caught up with distractions, hurt, and worries, but it's still there. We're wired for it. And when we connect with this purpose, it has the power to transform our lives.

The hardest part can be deciding to take the plunge. Wherever you are in your journey, look for a way to connect with the greater good, with a cause that is greater than the self-centric mazes of our mind. The world is waiting for you, eager to reach out and hold you, if you reach out for it. By looking beyond ourselves, we can unlock the door to realize inner growth – the only kind that really seems to matter when all is said and done.

It can be that simple.

Looking up at the clouds moving swiftly past, I start to walk again further east, past some willows and small blue flowers clustered low on the ground. Stooping down to see the flowers, I almost slip and sit in the mud, but catch myself, laughing, before I stand and start walking again. I've never reached the end of the trail, and I'm not sure where the path ends, but it doesn't really matter. For now, it's enough to take things step by step and see where the path leads me. As the wind flies rapidly past, I know that I might not see anyone around me, but I'm not really alone. I can feel it. There are many others headed the same way, looking for the same thing. Hope you can join us.

Building a New Life

How in the world did these people do it? And how can I?

That's what all of this makes me think. I have continually been amazed by all that these stories have to teach me, but I'm a pretty practical guy, so in addition to getting caught up in the stories in this book, a part of my mind is always wondering, "What does this mean for me?"

How did these 14 people reach beyond the problems that knocked them to the ground? I think it all boils down to decisions they made. It might seem like the world was making the decisions for them, but I believe that no matter what happened to these people or what happens to any of us, we have the power to decide where we will go and what we will do.

For these people, there were three key decisions.

The first decision they made was the decision to live.

This decision was stark for Rob, leukemia survivor, as he stood at the interstitial space between life and death, there at the train station, and saw his father inviting him to get on board – but he turned away. Alyssa held onto hope tightly, determined with all her spirit not to let her life slip away in the face of her cancer. The fires these people were scorched by may have made the decision easier, but still the decision was theirs. It could have gone either way.

Once these 14 people decided to live, the second thing they decided was how they see themselves. Having been through rough times, they could either see themselves as victims, or see themselves as potential creators in their own lives – regardless of whatever had happened in the past. We make this decision every day. Either life shapes us, or we shape our own lives, writing our own story.

Finally, once these individuals decided they were not a victim, their life was their own to decide and they had to decide what to do with it. Having decided to live a new life, they felt a deep need to live it well, to build a meaningful life connected to a purpose greater than their own life. For all that these people learned, this might be the greatest gift of all. By working to help others and connecting with the greater good, they also were healing their own lives along the way.

There's some strong science behind all this. When I talked with Jeff Bell, he directed me to The Center for the Greater Good at UC Berkeley, which is studying the power of purpose in our lives, finding how we can build better lives and a better society by working together. When we have a positive purpose we are contributing to, we feel good about ourselves. Our self esteem goes up, and we look forward to each day ahead. When that happens, a whole slew of mental and physical benefits follow. We break out of unhealthy thought patterns and our immune system gets stronger. We feel better, and we are better.

These stories show how invaluable it is to be optimistic and stay optimistic, to accept where we are but also to know that better things are ahead no matter how dark things seem today. Deciding to live, deciding to build a new life, and deciding to make a positive difference in the world – all these choices require optimism. When we believe life is a wonderful gift, this tends to be true. When we believe we can accomplish amazing things and make a positive difference in the world, we can. When we believe the opposite, then this also makes itself true for us. You've got to be willing to believe that you can live and do great things, no matter what the odds or other people say.

A clear mind is one factor that helped these 14 people successfully navigate their challenges to come out the other side. Our minds become overgrown with brush from all the years, an emotional and mental tangle that snarls at us, clutching at us, holding us back. Released from their old life, clearing away the overgrowth, these people were set free to begin a new life.

Take a step in this direction, clearing space in your mind for something new to grow. Maybe it comes through meditation, or taking a walk in the woods. Maybe sitting on the beach, or turning off the TV and sitting in a quiet room. We're so distracted by noise, words on screens, and the next rung on the ladder that we leave little room for anything else. We become so absorbed in ourselves and our own mind that we are no longer listening to each other, or to the deep well springs of creativity and creation that lie silently within.

Taking a move away from your old life isn't easy. In fact it can be scary as hell. Maybe you've thought about taking a step like this in your own life, but you held back, afraid. It's not unusual. Our natural tendency is often to stick to the safe path: to the people, places, and habits that we know. We might know that our old life isn't perfect, and we might want to change, but we hold back out of fear. It might not be easy, but we can do it. Even without having the universe force our hand, we can overcome our fear of moving down a new path if we believe in ourselves, and in the new life that lies ahead. If we release ourselves and accept the changes moving us away from our old life and toward a new one, it doesn't have to be that hard at all.

The stories these people have to offer about their lives are also an important part of what is going on here. We all have a story in our mind of who we are, a narrative that describes how we got to this point in our life and where we are going. Our minds are marvelous engines that constantly seek meaning, trying to make sense of our world and our lives. Sometimes these stories lead us astray. When we see ourselves as helpless victims, we tend to live this story out. By changing our story though, by changing how we see ourselves, we change our lives from the inside out. There's a growing field of Narrative Medicine that describes how this works, harnessing the healing power of belief. By listening to the stories of these survivors, we realize that we can follow in their footsteps to do the same. Through their inspiration, we can realize where our own stories have led us astray. And by rewriting the ending for our own story, we can redirect our own lives for the better, harnessing our own power to heal.

In her great book *"Dying to be Me"*, Anita Moorjani relates how a near-death experience showed her how she came to be riddled with cancer due to not accepting who she was. By accepting love, and by being the love that is within all of us, this vision showed her a new life moving forward. Almost overnight the cancer was cleared from her body. Miraculous is the only word for it. This power of vision, this ability to rewrite our own stories to have a new ending, lies within each of us.

Connecting with the greater good doesn't mean you need to be a saint or a spiritual leader, or that you need to be perfect. Nobody is, and holding perfection up as a goal can keep us from getting anywhere at all. You can find the greater good wherever you are and in whatever you do today. You can do it at work, taking care of business while also being a positive force in the world. You can do it in your community, joining groups and activities to help the elderly, the less fortunate, the environment, or other causes that need your help. You can volunteer at the senior center, or help the countless children around the world without enough food or water or education. Do it at home, with your own family, giving the people around you your time and your care. You'll feel better, and you'll find the energy you give will come back to you in surprising ways. The healing starts from right here and now if we're ready.

At the end of the day, I don't really think the answers to life are hidden away somewhere. We could spend our whole lives searching the globe for the key to a better and more meaningful life and never find it, because it's not hidden in a secret far-off castle. It is found inside ourselves and in each other, and it's been there all the time. All we have to do is open our eyes and allow ourselves to see.

Appendix: Resources

Chapter 1: Rob Meadows

Rob Meadows is the founder of Gifts from the Train Station, where the stories of explorers like those in this book are offered to help others in their own journey. You can get in touch with Rob at the website, make a donation, tell your own story, find ways to help others, and get inspired by others who've been knocked down and got back up to do great things. Go to:

www.GiftsFromtheTrainStation.org

Chapter 2: Mark Black

Mark travels across North America inspiring people with his story and lessons from his experiences that can help others overcome their own challenges, no matter how formidable they appear. Mark's book *"Living Life from the Heart"* is available on Amazon or other booksellers, and also at his website. To get in touch with Mark and find out about his availability as a speaker for events and success coach, go to:

www.MarkBlackSpeaks.com

Chapter 3: Dr. Alice Chan

Dr. Alice Chan delivers workshops, seminars, and coaching programs with a unique REACH approach helping others to find their purpose in life and make it happen. Her book *"REACH Your Dreams: Five Steps to be a Conscious Creator in Your Life"* is available on Amazon and other booksellers, and you can reach Dr. Chan and find out more how she can help at:

www.dralicechan.com

Chapter 4: Roger Wright

Roger Wright keeps on running, inspiring people everywhere with his example, and helping his niece and the many others affected by cystic fibrosis. You can contact Roger, make a contribution to his current efforts, and find out more about his story at:

www.runningformyexistence.com or www.RFME.org

Chapter 5: Dr. Nicole Eastman

Dr. Nicole Eastman is working on a book about her experiences, writing, speaking, and reaching out to others who have dealt with trauma and tragedy, and need help reaching beyond it. To find out more about Dr. Eastman and get in touch with her, go to:

www.drnicolemeastman.com

Chapter 6: Mel Brake

Through Mel's Poetry Works, Mel Brake continues working with disadvantaged children, helping them to find their voice, to know they are valuable. You can read his work and find out about events at:

http://melbrake.wordpress.com/

Chapter 7: Mailet Lopez

Mailet Lopez is working with IHadCancer.com to help more people with cancer to reach out and make the connections they deeply need. To get in touch with her, find help for your own struggle with cancer, and connect with others who need the same, go to:

www.IHadCancer.com

Chapter 8: Brooke Miller

Brooke Miller continues working through Soapbox Therapy to improve mental health through her practice, blog, and other outreach, providing grounded, insightful, and accessible help for the great many people who need it. To get in touch with her, and find out the latest about all she is involved with, go to:

www.soapboxtherapy.com

Chapter 9: Julie Gallegos

Julie Gallegos is growing her business and her new life with WhatChyaGot Bags, helping more people to have good lives even when they are facing difficult physical challenges. To find out more about Julie and the WhatChyaGot Bag, go to:

www.whatchyagotbags.com

Chapter 10: Dave Alberga

As the CEO of Active Network, Dave Alberga remains a busy man, but also one with a clear purpose in life that's bigger than the bottom line. In addition to fighting IBD through his work with the Crohn's and Colitis Foundation (www.cfa.org), he's taking on the even bigger challenge of encouraging fitness and health. Be sure to follow his progress at:

www.Activenetwork.com

Chapter 11: Crissy Saint

Crissy Saint is moving past her tragedy and turmoil, and building a new life of purpose. She writes eloquently and with disarming candor on her blog, where she can be reached at:

www.crissysaint.wordpress.com/

Chapter 12: Christine Clifford

Christine Clifford is a busy woman tackling multiple causes, giving people hope and humor in difficult times. To get in touch with her, read more, find help in dealing with cancer or divorce, or to reach out and help others, I'm sure Christine would love hearing from you at:

www.cancerclub.com and

www.divorcingdivas.com

Chapter 13: Alyssa Phillips

After beating the odds in her fight with cancer, Alyssa is a walking miracle, with some amazing things ahead in the new life she's embracing. Be sure to check her site for the latest on her upcoming book and events at:

www.alyssaphillipsinc.com

Chapter 14: Jeff Bell

In finding how to manage his own OCD by focusing on the Greater Good, Jeff Bell ended up helping not just himself, but other OCD sufferers, and people everywhere facing their own challenges in life. We do best in life when we have a purpose larger than our own lives. Jeff has written two books that are excellent resources and available at booksellers everywhere, including:

"*Rewind, Replay, Repeat: A Memoir of Obsessive Compulsive Disorder*", describing his own life overcoming his OCD.

"*When in Doubt, Make Belief: An OCD-Inspired Approach to Living with Uncertainty*", which is an inspiring and useful book for people to connect with the Greater Good in their lives, not just to deal with OCD but many other challenges.

You can also read more about the Adversity 2 Advocacy project, harnessing the power of the Greater Good Perspective Shift for people with many challenges at:

www.adversity2advocacy.org

The Greater Good Science Center provides more information about the science and practical applications for people looking for purpose and health in their lives at: http://greatergood.berkeley.edu/

The International OCD Foundation: To get help with OCD, or to offer help to others, go to: http://www.ocfoundation.org/

Photo Credits

Images are used courtesy of the following:

Introduction: Glenn Croston

Chapter 1: Rob Meadows

Chapter 2: Mark Black

Chapter 3: Alice Chan

Chapter 4: Roger Wright

Chapter 5: Nicole Eastman

Chapter 6: Mel Brake

Chapter 7: Mailet Lopez

Chapter 8: Brooke Miller

Chapter 9: Julie Gallegos

Chapter 10: Dave Alberga

Chapter 11: Crissy Saint

Chapter 12: Christine Clifford

Chapter 13: Alyssa Phillips, photo by Marie Thomas

Chapter 14: Jeff Bell

Conclusion: Glenn Croston

About the Author

Glenn Croston is a PhD scientist, author, and dad. Previously he has written "*75 Green Businesses You Can Start to Make Money and Make a Difference*" and "*Starting Green: An Ecopreneur's Toolkit for Starting a Green Business from Business Plan to Profits*", describing how anyone can build a business that has a positive impact on the world. He is also the author of "*The Real Story of Risk: Adventures in a Hazardous World*" (October 2012), describing how our human roots shape and bend how we see the many risks of our world. Currently residing in San Diego, Glenn is always looking forward to hearing your story. He can be reached any time at www.startingupgreen.com, or at www.giftsfromthetrainstation.org.

www.ingramcontent.com/pod-product-compliance
Lightning Source LLC
Chambersburg PA
CBHW060508030426
42337CB00015B/1801